Let them eat cake!

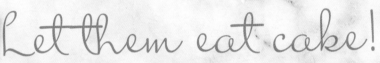

WELCOME TO PRIMA'S THE JOY OF BAKING, a collection of 139 of our best recipes for bread, biscuits, savouries and cakes of every description — big, small, fruity, chocolate, iced, plain — but all utterly, lip-smackingly delicious!

Of course, it's *The Great British Bake Off* that has made so many of us obsessed with baking in recent years — the ultimate TV recipe of different personalities pitched in competition, lifted by some learning along the way and a dollop of humour. It's great entertainment and, despite the odd soggy bottom and decorating disaster, most of the results *do* look good enough to eat. We can rest assured that everything will turn out fine at the end of the show, with smiles all round and big slices of gorgeous sponge.

And I guess that is what's at the heart of the show's popularity and, indeed, the nation's rekindled love of baking. At a time when so many of us spend so much of our lives in front of screens — and increasingly communicate via email, texts and social media — baking provides a fantastic hands-on, sensory experience. In a short time, you can create something divine from just a handful of ingredients to share with family and friends. And this is the kind of sharing that you can't possibly do via Twitter or Facebook; doling out slices of cake and getting together for afternoon tea can only be done in person, face-to-face. There really is only one word for it: joy!

Gaby

GABY HUDDART, **EDITOR-IN-CHIEF**

More of what you love from Prima every day at

prima.co.uk

Recipes

TRY OUR MIDWEEK MEALS WHEN YOU'RE SHORT ON TIME, PLUS DON'T MISS OUR ULTIMATE GUIDE TO MAKING ICE CREAM!

Newsletter

GET THE BEST STORIES OF THE WEEK, STRAIGHT TO YOUR INBOX, PLUS EXCITING OFFERS AND COMPETITIONS! SIGN UP TODAY AT PRIMA.CO.UK/NEWSLETTER.

Crafts

FIND SIMPLE CRAFT PROJECTS TO MAKE WITH THE KIDS, INSPIRING UPCYCLING TIPS TO REV UP YOUR FURNITURE AND EVERYTHING YOU NEED TO KNOW ABOUT DECOUPAGE!

JOIN OUR BOOK CLUB!
LOVE READING? REVIEW OUR BOOK OF THE MONTH AND JOIN THE DISCUSSION

SHOP WITH US!
SNAP UP DISCOUNTED WOOLS AND YARNS IN OUR CRAFT SHOP

BECOME A FAN
SEE THE LATEST FROM PRIMA ON YOUR FACEBOOK NEWSFEED AND NEVER MISS ANOTHER STORY

VISIT PRIMA.CO.UK TODAY!

12

36

20

40

Classics

46 TINY ÉCLAIRS
48 RASPBERRY + ALMOND FRIAND
50 RASPBERRY CREAM SLICES
52 BLACKBERRY + APPLE SCONE CAKE
54 CHERRY BAKEWELLS
56 HOT CROSS BUN LOAF
58 VANILLA SPONGE WITH LEMON CURD
60 LEMON TARTLETS
62 EXTRA SPECIAL GINGER SPONGE
64 COCONUT CAKE
66 APPLE + CINNAMON MINI SCONES
68 FONDANT FANCIES
70 TUNIS CAKE
72 LEMON DRIZZLE BARS
74 COFFEE + WALNUT SPONGE
76 STRIPY ROCK RED VELVET
78 LEMON + HONEY BUNDT
80 DAISY SWISS ROLL
82 PEANUT BUTTER CHEESECAKE

80

60

46

58

Cupcakes

10 COCONUT + LIME CUPCAKES
12 SUMMER BERRY + MASCARPONE
14 SPRING FLOWER TEATIME TREAT
16 CHOCOLATE + CREAMY BLACKBERRY
18 BITE-SIZE, PRETTY FLORAL
20 ROSE + WHITE CHOCOLATE BOUQUET
22 BLUEBERRY + LEMON TOFFEE
24 MINTY CHOCOLATE
26 PEANUT BUTTER CHOC CHIP
28 LEMON SHERBET CHICKS
30 BUTTERCREAM FLOWER FAVOURITES
32 COFFEE + WALNUT CLASSIC
34 PINK + WHITE MARSHMALLOW TOPPING
36 MACARON-TOPPED ALMOND CAKE
38 CHOCOLATE POP CANDY CAKES
40 ICED VIOLA FAIRY CAKE
42 SHADES OF PINK
44 CHOCOLATE + RASPBERRY ROSEBUD

84

94

90

112

Chocolate

84 HIDDEN HEART CAKE
86 CHOCOLATE + CRANBERRY FLAPJACKS
88 CHOCOLATE FINGER FUDGE CAKE
90 CHOCOLATE TARTS WITH BLACKBERRIES
92 STRIPY RASPBERRY GATEAU
94 WHITE TRUFFLE CAKE EGGS
96 CHOCOLATE TOFFEE POPCORN CAKE
98 MERINGUE MERVEILLEUX
100 BRANDIED PRUNE MARQUISE
102 MEGA CHOCOLATE TRAY BAKE
104 APRICOT, ALMOND + WHITE CHOC LOAF
106 CHOCOLATE ECLAIRS
108 CHEESECAKE-SWIRLED BROWNIES
110 CHOC + CRUSHED VIOLET MADELEINES
112 CARAMEL BROWNIE HEART
114 BLACK FOREST SLICE
116 PRALINE LAYER CAKE
118 CHOCOLATE TARTLETS
120 CHOCOLATE MERINGUE ROULADE
122 CHOCOLATE BRANDY PROFITEROLES
124 CARDAMOM CHOCOLATE TORTE
126 CHOCOLATE, CHERRY + PISTACHIO FUDGE

Savoury

128 SHORTCRUST PASTRY
129 CRAB + WATERCRESS SUMMER TART
130 CHEAT'S PORK PIES
132 HAM, SPINACH + STILTON TART
134 SPINACH, BACON + CHEESE SCONES
136 PEPPER + GOATS' CHEESE TART
138 CORNISH PASTIES
140 RAISIN + CARAWAY SEED BREAD
142 ASPARAGUS + CHEESE TART
144 PIZZA SWIRLS
146 CARAMELISED ONION + GARLIC TART
148 PEPPER PUFF PIE
150 RED PEPPER + PROSCIUTTO STROMBOLI
152 SUNBLUSH TOMATO FOCACCIA
154 SMOKED FISH + BABY LEEK FLAN
156 OLIVE + CHEESE BREADSTICKS
158 COURGETTE + PINE NUT TART
160 HOME-MADE CHEESE PRETZELS
162 BUTTERNUT SQUASH + SAGE TART
164 DATE + WALNUT WHEATEN BREAD
166 POLENTA + CHORIZO BUNS

128

150

160

130

198

196

170

208

Biscuits

212 PASTEL MACARONS
214 SHORTBREAD FINGERS
216 VANILLA CREAM OREOS
218 SHORTBREAD FLOWERS
220 CHOCOLATE, CHERRY + NUT BISCUITS
222 GIANT CELEBRATION COOKIE CAKE
224 VIENNESE BISCUITS
226 CHOCOLATE CHIP COOKIES
228 PISTACHIO BISCOTTI
230 WHITE CHOC + CRANBERRY COOKIES
232 ICED BISCUITS
234 RASPBERRY CREAMS
236 CHOCOLATE + ALMOND CHEWY BARS
238 LAVENDER + BORAGE GARLANDS
240 CRANBERRY + COCONUT SQUARES
242 GINGERBREAD PEOPLE
244 FEATHERED SHORTBREAD HEARTS
246 ENGLISH MACAROONS
248 CHOC-DIPPED SHORTBREAD SQUARES
250 HONEY + OAT FLAPJACK COOKIES

Special occasions

168 ALLOTMENT CARROT CAKE
170 ALMOND CAKE FLOWER GARLAND
172 LEMON + ROSEMARY LOAF
174 BUTTERCREAM ROSE CAKE
176 FLOWER POT CAKES
178 COTTAGE CAKE
180 CELEBRATION CAKE
182 EASTER BUNNY BISCUIT CAKE
184 CUCKOO CLOCK CAKE
186 DAISY CAKE
188 CUTE KITTY CAKE
190 HYDRANGEA CAKE
192 LACE-TRIMMED CAKE
194 MINI MERINGUE MOUTHFULS
196 PISTACHIO, LIME + ROSE ICED LOAF
198 RAINBOW MERINGUE LAYERS
200 RASPBERRY LAYER CAKE
202 RASPBERRY, REDCURRANT + ROSE SPONGE
204 RUFFLE CAKE
206 INDIVIDUAL ICED CAKES
208 BLOSSOM + BUTTERFLY CAKE
210 GIANT MARSHMALLOW CRISPY CAKE

212

222

242

218

CONTENTS

254

272

280

264

Christmas

252 **CHELSEA BUN CHRISTMAS TREE**

254 **CHOCOLATE BOMBE**

256 **CHOC, GINGER + CHERRY GARLAND**

258 **REINDEER CAKE CUBES**

260 **GIFT PARCEL CAKES**

262 **CHRISTMAS TREE CAKE**

264 **CRANBERRY ROULADE**

266 **FONDANT FANCIES**

268 **GINGERBREAD ADVENT CALENDAR**

270 **GOLD HOLLY CUPCAKES**

272 **CHOCOLATE-DECORATED LEBKUCHEN**

274 **LEMON + COCONUT SNOWBALLS**

276 **LET IT SNOW CAKE**

278 **MERINGUE TREES**

280 **MINI GINGERBREAD BIRD HOUSES**

282 **MINI PANETTONES**

284 **ORANGE + CRANBERRY HEART**

286 **ROCKY ROAD CHUNKS**

The joy of BAKING

Published by Hearst Magazines UK,
72 Broadwick Street, London W1F 9EP.
Tel: 020 7439 5000. Email: prima@hearst.co.uk

Editor-in-chief **Gaby Huddart**
Editor **Sue McNeill**
Art editors **Terry Wallace** and **Ruth Mcann**
Chief sub editor **Tracy Müller-King**
PA **Sandra Tear**
Picture editor **Jo Lockwood**

Group publishing director **Sharon Douglas**
Circulation manager **James Hill**
Marketing manager **Charlotte Cunliffe**
Production manager **Pavel Pachovsky**
Advertising production controller **Jonathan Stuart**
Lifestyle commercial finance manager **Naina Savraj**

Chief executive officer **Anna Jones**
Managing director, Brands **Michael Rowley**
Group commercial director **Ella Dolphin**
Chief technical officer **Darren Goldsby**
Strategy and product director **Lee Wilkinson**
Marketing and circulation director **Reid Holland**
Director of communications **Lisa Quinn**
SVP, Chief financial officer and general manager
Hearst Magazines International **Simon Horne**
President and chief executive officer
Hearst Magazines International **Duncan Edwards**

Advertising **020 7439 5000**
Distribution **01895 433 600**
Switchboard **020 7439 5000**
Subscriptions/back issues **01858 438 844**
email: **hearst@subscription.co.uk**

HEARST *magazines* UK

Become our Facebook friend at
facebook.com/primamagazine

Share what you love at
pinterest.com/primamagazine

Find out what's going on here at Prima
by following us on Twitter: @primamag

The joy of CUPCAKES

These eye-catching cakes are ideal for afternoon tea, a birthday celebration or to give as a gift

Coconut + lime CUPCAKES

These have a delicious zesty flavour, and can even be made a bit boozy by adding 1 tablespoon of rum or coconut liqueur to the syrup

MAKES 12 **PREP TIME** 30 MINS **BAKE** 25 MINS

FOR THE SPONGE
- 125g butter, softened
- 125g caster sugar
- 3 medium eggs, beaten
- 125g self-raising flour
- 25g desiccated coconut
- Zest of 1 lime

FOR THE SYRUP
- Juice of 1 lime
- 25g caster sugar

FOR THE ICING
- 280g pack full-fat cream cheese
- 150g icing sugar
- 300ml double cream
- Zest of 1 lime

YOU WILL NEED
- A 12-hole cupcake tin, lined with paper cases
- A pastry brush
- A plastic piping bag

★ Preheat oven to gas mark 4/180°C (160°C in a fan oven).

★ **TO MAKE SPONGE,** place butter and sugar in a mixing bowl and beat until light, creamy and pale in colour. Gradually add eggs, beating well after each addition. If mixture curdles, add a spoonful of flour. Lightly stir in the remaining flour and the coconut and lime zest until evenly mixed.

★ Divide mixture between cupcake cases and bake for 20-25 mins until golden and firm to the touch.

★ Meanwhile, make the syrup. Pour lime juice into a pan and add sugar. Bring to the boil and cook for 1 min to thicken it slightly. Brush mixture over top of cakes when they come out of the oven. Leave to cool in tin for 5 mins then turn out on to a wire rack to cool.

★ **TO MAKE ICING,** beat together cream cheese and icing sugar until smooth, then add cream and whisk until thick enough to pipe. Place in a piping bag and snip off the end to make a 1cm hole. Pipe swirls of icing on to cupcakes and decorate with lime zest.

RECIPE, FOOD AND PROP STYLING: MITZIE WILSON **PHOTO**: DAN JONES

Summer berry +
MASCARPONE

*Sugar-frosted summer berries and a rich mascarpone topping transform
a simple sponge recipe into a gorgeous treat*

MAKES 12 **PREP** 30 MINS **BAKE** 25 MINS

FOR THE SPONGE

- 150g butter, at room temperature
- 150g golden caster sugar
- 3 medium eggs, beaten
- 150g self-raising flour
- ½tsp vanilla extract

FOR THE TOPPING

- 200g mascarpone
- ½tsp vanilla extract
- 1tsp icing sugar to decorate
- A few raspberries and blueberries
- 1 egg white, beaten (optional)
- 2tbsp caster sugar (optional)
- Mint sprigs, to serve

YOU WILL NEED

- A 12-hole cupcake tin, lined with paper cases
- A pastry brush

★ Preheat oven to gas mark 4/180°C (160°C in a fan oven).

★ Place butter and sugar in a mixing bowl and beat with a wooden spoon or electric whisk until the butter becomes pale and the mixture is light and fluffy.

★ Add eggs, a little at a time, beating well after each addition. Add 1-2tbsp flour, if necessary, to prevent mixture curdling. Fold in the remaining flour and the vanilla with a large metal spoon.

★ Divide mixture between the cupcake cases and bake for 20-25 mins until golden brown and just firm to the touch. Remove cupcakes from tin and leave to cool completely on a wire rack.

★ **TO MAKE ICING,** whip together mascarpone, vanilla extract and icing sugar, then spread over the cupcakes.

★ **TO SUGAR-COAT BERRIES,** lightly brush each one with egg white, then roll in caster sugar. Arrange a few on top of each cake with a sprig of mint. (Once 'frosted', fruit will only keep for 1 hr, so decorate cakes at the last minute or omit sugar frosting and top with fresh berries instead.)

RECIPE, FOOD AND PROP STYLING: MITZIE WILSON **PHOTO:** CLIVE STREETER

Spring flower
TEATIME TREAT

These vanilla cakes are made extra special with pretty sugar paste flowers

MAKES 12 **PREP** 1 HR, PLUS OVERNIGHT DRYING **BAKE** 25 MINS

RECIPE, FOOD AND PROP STYLING: MITZIE WILSON **PHOTO:** CLIVE BOZZARD-HILL PHOTOGRAPHY

FOR THE FLOWERS
- 100g sugar paste
- Concentrated paste food colourings in desired shades

FOR THE SPONGE
- 150g butter, softened
- 150g caster sugar
- 3 medium eggs, beaten
- 150g self-raising flour
- ½tsp vanilla extract

FOR THE TOPPING
- 150g butter, softened
- 350g icing sugar, plus extra, for dusting
- ½tsp vanilla extract

YOU WILL NEED
- Blossom, daisy and primrose flower cutters
- A small butterfly cutter
- A 12-hole cupcake tin, lined with paper cases
- A large piping bag and star nozzle

★ It's best to make the sugar paste flowers the day before the cakes. Divide and colour the sugar paste as desired, then roll out very thinly, 1 piece at a time, on a work surface dusted with icing sugar. Cut out flowers and butterflies and leave for 24 hours in a dry place on crumpled kitchen paper. They will keep for up to 3 months in an airtight container.

★ Preheat oven to gas mark 4/180°C (160°C in a fan oven).

★ In a bowl, beat together butter and sugar with a wooden spoon or electric whisk until really light and fluffy. Gradually add eggs, a little at a time, beating well after each addition – add a little flour if the mixture begins to curdle. Beat in the remaining flour and the vanilla extract.

★ Divide mixture between cupcake cases and bake for 20-25 mins until golden brown and firm to the touch. Remove cakes from tin and leave to cool on a wire rack.

★ **TO DECORATE,** beat together butter, icing sugar and vanilla until soft and creamy. Place in a piping bag fitted with a star-shaped nozzle and pipe on to the cupcakes. Decorate with the sugar paste flowers just before serving.

Chocolate + creamy
BLACKBERRY

This is a delicious combo, but if you prefer plain cupcakes, simply swap the cocoa for self-raising flour and add half a teaspoon of vanilla extract

MAKES 12 **PREP** 30 MINS **BAKE** 25 MINS

FOR THE SPONGE

- 150g butter, at room temperature
- 150g golden caster sugar
- 3 medium eggs, beaten
- 125g self-raising flour
- 25g cocoa powder, sifted
- 100g blackberries

FOR THE TOPPING

- 150ml double cream
- 150g blackberries
- 1tsp icing sugar
- A few mint leaves

YOU WILL NEED

- A 12-hole cupcake tin, lined with paper cases

★ Preheat oven to gas mark 4/180°C (160°C in a fan oven).

★ Place butter and sugar in a mixing bowl and beat with a wooden spoon or electric whisk until butter is a pale colour and the mixture is light and fluffy.

★ Add eggs, a little at a time, beating well after each addition. Add 1 or 2tbsp flour, if necessary, to prevent mixture curdling. Using a large metal spoon, fold in the remaining flour with the cocoa powder and blackberries.

★ Divide mixture between cupcake cases and bake for 20-25 mins until golden brown and just firm to the touch. Remove cupcakes from tin and leave to cool on a wire rack.

★ **TO DECORATE,** whip cream until it just holds its shape, then mash in half of the blackberries and sweeten with icing sugar. Spoon a little on to each cupcake and top with a few of the remaining blackberries and a sprig of mint.

RECIPE AND FOOD STYLING: MITZIE WILSON PROP STYLING: SUE ROWLANDS PHOTO: CLIVE BOZZARD-HILL PHOTOGRAPHY

Try this
Add half a chopped apple to the mix, if you like – it's a classic with blackberries.

Bite-size, pretty FLORAL

Cupcakes make a lovely gift presented in a pretty box lined with tissue paper

MAKES 24 **PREP** 30 MINS **BAKE** 15 MINS

FOR THE SPONGE

- 150g butter, at room temperature
- 150g golden caster sugar
- ½tsp vanilla extract
- 3 medium eggs, beaten
- 150g self-raising flour

FOR THE TOPPING

- 75g butter, softened
- 150g icing sugar
- Assorted royal icing sugar flowers

YOU WILL NEED

- 2 x 12-hole mini cupcake tins, lined with mini paper cases
- A piping bag with star nozzle

★ Preheat oven to gas mark 4/180˚C (160˚C in a fan oven).

★ Place butter, sugar and vanilla extract in a mixing bowl and beat with a wooden spoon or electric whisk until the butter becomes a pale colour and the mixture is light and fluffy.

★ Add eggs, a little at a time, beating well after each addition. Add 1-2tbsp flour, if necessary, to prevent the mixture curdling, then fold in the remaining flour with a large metal spoon.

★ Divide mixture between cupcake cases and bake for about 12 mins until golden brown and just firm to the touch. Remove cakes from tin and allow to cool completely on a wire rack.

★ **TO DECORATE,** first make the icing by whisking or beating together the butter and icing sugar with 1-2tsp boiling water until really light and creamy. Place in a piping bag and pipe it in swirls on top of the cakes, then add a few sugar flowers.

RECIPE, FOOD AND PROP STYLING: MITZIE WILSON PHOTO: CLARE WINFIELD

Rose + white chocolate
BOUQUET

A pretty-as-a-picture 'bouquet' of cupcakes

MAKES 12 **PREP** 1 HR **BAKE** 25 MINS

FOR THE SPONGE
- 75g white chocolate
- 100g caster sugar
- 100g butter, softened
- 2 eggs
- 125g self-raising flour
- 1tsp vanilla extract

FOR THE TOPPING
- 200g white chocolate
- 200g unsalted butter
- 1tsp rose water, to taste
- A little green and pink food colouring

YOU WILL NEED
- A 12-hole cupcake tray, lined with paper cases
- 2 plastic piping bags and 1 large star nozzle

★ Preheat oven to gas mark 4/180°C (160°C in a fan oven).

★ Chop the chocolate, add to a food processor with half the sugar and whizz until finely chopped. Add 2tbsp hot water, blend again, then add the remaining sponge ingredients and whizz again until mixed together.

★ Divide mixture between cupcake cases and bake for 20-25 mins until golden and firm. Remove cakes from tin and leave to cool on a wire rack.

★ **TO DECORATE,** chop chocolate and add to a bowl set over a pan of simmering water (don't let it touch the water). Beat butter until soft, then add melted chocolate and beat until smooth. Add rose water to your liking, then chill the icing, if necessary, until thick enough to pipe.

★ Colour 3-4tbsp icing with green food colouring and set aside. Colour the rest of the icing with pink food colouring and place in a piping bag fitted with a star nozzle. Pipe a swirl on each cake (reserve a little for the bow), and arrange them on a board, as shown (right).

★ Place green icing in second piping bag, snip off the end, and pipe 'flower stems' on to the board. Using the reserved pink buttercream, pipe a bow over the stems.

RECIPE, FOOD AND PROP STYLING: MITZIE WILSON **PHOTO:** CLARE WINFIELD

Try this

Rose water can vary in strength, so add to taste. The cakes will keep in a tin for 2-3 days.

Blueberry + lemon TOFFEE

A lovely combination – we've used dark muscovado sugar to give a deeper flavour, but you can use white caster sugar, if you prefer

MAKES 12   **PREP** 30 MINS   **BAKE** 25 MINS

RECIPE, FOOD AND PROP STYLING: MITZIE WILSON **PHOTO:** CLIVE BOZZARD-HILL PHOTOGRAPHY

FOR THE SPONGE
- 150g butter, at room temperature
- 150g dark muscovado sugar
- 3 medium eggs, beaten
- 150g self-raising flour
- ½tsp baking powder
- Zest of 1 unwaxed lemon

FOR THE TOPPING
- 100g butter, softened
- 150g full-fat cream cheese
- 150g icing sugar, sifted
- Fresh blueberries, to decorate
- A few sprigs of mint, to decorate (optional)

YOU WILL NEED
- A 12-hole cupcake tin, lined with paper cases

★ Preheat oven to gas mark 4/180ºC (160ºC in a fan oven).

★ Place butter and sugar in a mixing bowl and beat with a wooden spoon or electric whisk until butter becomes a pale colour and the mixture is light and fluffy.

★ Add eggs, a little at a time, beating well after each addition. Add 1-2tbsp flour, if necessary, to prevent mixture curdling, then fold in the remaining flour and the baking powder and lemon zest.

★ Divide mixture between cupcake cases and bake for 20-25 mins until golden brown and just firm to the touch. Remove cakes from tin and leave to cool completely on a wire rack.

★ **TO DECORATE,** beat butter until smooth, then gradually stir in cream cheese until well combined. Add icing sugar and beat well until smooth. Spread on top of cakes and decorate with blueberries and mint sprigs.

Minty CHOCOLATE

You can ring the changes by topping with honeycomb balls or chocolate buttons instead of the mint chocolate bubbles

MAKES 12 **PREP** 30 MINS **BAKE** 25 MINS

FOR THE SPONGE

- 150g butter, at room temperature
- 150g golden caster sugar
- 3 medium eggs, beaten
- 115g self-raising flour
- 35g cocoa powder, sifted
- 2 drops of peppermint extract (optional)

FOR THE TOPPING

- 75ml double cream
- 150g milk chocolate, finely chopped or grated
- 1 bag chocolate mint Aero Bubbles, roughly chopped (optional)

YOU WILL NEED

- A 12-hole muffin tin, lined with paper cupcake cases

★ Preheat oven to gas mark 4/180°C (160°C in a fan oven).

★ Beat butter and sugar in a mixing bowl with a wooden spoon or electric whisk until butter becomes a pale colour and the mixture is light and fluffy.

★ Add eggs, a little at a time, beating well after each addition. Add 1-2tbsp flour, if necessary, to prevent mixture curdling, then fold in the remaining flour, as well as the cocoa and peppermint extract (if using), with a large metal spoon.

★ Divide mixture between cupcake cases and bake for 20-25 mins until golden brown. Remove cakes from tin and leave to cool completely on a wire rack.

★ **TO DECORATE,** warm cream in a small pan until hot, then add chocolate and stir until smooth and completely melted. Leave to cool in the fridge until thick, then spread over the cupcakes and decorate with mint chocolate bubbles.

RECIPE, FOOD AND PROP STYLING: MITZIE WILSON **PHOTO:** CLIVE STREETER

Peanut butter CHOC CHIP

These are utterly addictive! Omit the choc chips, if you like

MAKES 12 **PREP** 30 MINS **BAKE** 25 MINS

FOR THE SPONGE
- 100g butter, at room temperature
- 200g self-raising flour
- 200g light muscovado sugar
- 1tsp baking powder
- 150g crunchy peanut butter
- 3 large eggs
- 100ml milk
- 100g plain chocolate chips

FOR THE TOPPING
- 50g peanut butter
- 25g butter, softened
- 200g icing sugar, sifted
- 50g salted peanuts
- A few chocolate sprinkles

YOU WILL NEED
- A 12-hole cupcake tin, lined with paper cases

★ Preheat oven to gas mark 4/180°C (160°C in a fan oven).

★ Place all the sponge ingredients into a large mixing bowl and beat with a wooden spoon until well mixed.

★ Divide mixture between cupcake cases and bake for 20-25 mins until golden brown and just firm to the touch. Remove cakes from tin and leave to cool completely on a wire rack.

★ **TO DECORATE,** beat together peanut butter, butter and icing sugar with 1tsp boiling water until smooth. Spread a little on top of each cupcake and top with peanuts and chocolate sprinkles.

RECIPE, FOOD AND PROP STYLING: MITZIE WILSON **PHOTO:** TOBY SCOTT

Lemon sherbet CHICKS

Packed with citrussy flavour, these cakes will be a hit with little ones

MAKES 12 **PREP** 1 HR **BAKE** 25 MINS

FOR THE SPONGE
- 150g butter, softened
- 150g caster sugar
- 3 medium eggs, beaten
- 150g self-raising flour
- Zest of 1 lemon and 2tbsp juice

FOR THE LEMON SHERBET
- 100g granulated sugar
- Zest of 1 lemon
- 1tsp citric acid (optional – available from a chemist)
- Yellow food colouring

FOR THE TOPPING
- 150g butter, softened
- 350g icing sugar
- A drop of vanilla extract
- A little sugar paste
- Brown and orange food colouring

YOU WILL NEED
- A 12-hole cupcake tin, lined with paper cases

★ Preheat oven to gas mark 4/180°C (160°C in a fan oven).

★ Beat together butter and sugar in a mixing bowl with a wooden spoon or electric whisk until really light and fluffy. Gradually add eggs, a little at a time, beating well – add a little flour if the mixture begins to curdle. Beat in the flour, lemon zest and juice.

★ Divide mixture between cupcake cases and bake for 20-25 mins until golden brown and firm to the touch. Remove cakes from tin and leave to cool on a wire rack.

★ **TO MAKE LEMON SHERBET,** mix sugar with lemon zest and citric acid, if using. Add a little yellow food colouring and stir together until evenly coloured.

★ **TO ICE CAKES,** beat together butter, icing sugar and vanilla until soft. Spread over cakes, making it slightly domed then, holding cakes upside down, dip icing into the sherbet.

★ **TO DECORATE,** make eyes for chicks by rolling sugar paste into small balls and flatten slightly, if you like, then dot with brown food colouring to make 'pupils'. Colour a little sugar paste with orange food colouring, then cut out beaks and feet and press on to the cakes. Colour another small batch of sugar paste with yellow food colouring and mould into short 'feathers'. Press these on to the 'heads' of the chicks, then arrange cupcakes in a nest of tissue paper strips, if you like.

RECIPE, FOOD AND PROP STYLING: MITZIE WILSON **PHOTO:** TOBY SCOTT

Try this
Mastering the rose technique takes a little practice, but the results are stunning.

★HYDRANGEAS

★PRIMROSES

★ROSES

Buttercream flower
FAVOURITES

Make these pretty floral-themed cakes using multi-hued buttercreams and different piping nozzles

MAKES 12   **PREP** 1 HR   **BAKE** 25 MINS

RECIPE AND FOOD STYLING: MITZIE WILSON **PROP STYLING:** SUE ROWLANDS **PHOTO:** TOBY SCOTT

FOR THE SPONGE
- 150g butter, at room temperature
- 150g caster sugar
- 3 medium eggs, beaten
- 150g self-raising flour

FOR THE TOPPING
- 100g butter
- 250g icing sugar
- Blue, pink and yellow food colouring

YOU WILL NEED
- A 12-hole cupcake tin, lined with paper cases
- 3 piping bags
- A large open-star piping nozzle
- A medium petal nozzle

★ Preheat oven to gas mark 4/180°C (160°C in a fan oven).

★ Place butter and sugar in a mixing bowl and beat with a wooden spoon or electric whisk until light and fluffy. Gradually beat in eggs, a little at a time, until smooth, adding a little flour if mixture curdles. Stir in the rest of the flour until smooth.

★ Spoon mixture into cupcake cases and bake for 20-25 mins until golden brown and just firm to the touch. Remove cupcakes from tin and leave to cool on a wire rack.

★ **TO MAKE TOPPING,** place butter in a bowl with 2tsp boiling water, then add icing sugar and beat until smooth. Divide icing between 3 bowls and add a different food colouring to each.

★ **TO MAKE HYDRANGEAS,** spread a little yellow icing down one side of a piping bag fitted with a star nozzle, then fill the bag with blue icing and pipe stars, packed closely together, on to 4 cupcakes.

★ **TO MAKE ROSES,** place pink icing into a piping bag fitted with a petal nozzle. Place thick end of nozzle against cake and pipe a bud in the centre, turning the cake rather than the nozzle. Pipe petals around bud, placing nozzle flat against cake, then turning it up and over to make each petal, while turning the cake. Do this on 4 cupcakes.

★ **TO MAKE PRIMROSES,** place yellow icing into a piping bag fitted with a petal nozzle and pipe 5 or 6 petals in a circle on last 4 cupcakes. You should pipe petals as if piping a loop.

Coffee + walnut CLASSIC

The old favourite teatime cake has been reworked into a delicious cupcake

MAKES 12 **PREP** 30 MINS **BAKE** 25 MINS

FOR THE SPONGE

- 75g walnuts
- 150g butter, at room temperature
- 150g light muscovado sugar
- 3 medium eggs, beaten
- 125g self-raising flour
- 2tsp instant coffee
- ½tsp baking powder

FOR THE TOPPING

- 50g butter, softened
- 150g icing sugar
- 25g walnut pieces

YOU WILL NEED

- A 12-hole muffin tin, lined with paper cases

★ Preheat oven to gas mark 4/180°C (160°C in a fan oven).

★ Finely chop walnuts in a food processor, but be careful not to whizz them to a powder. Reserve 1tbsp for icing.

★ Beat butter and sugar in a bowl with a wooden spoon or electric whisk until butter turns a pale colour and the mixture is fluffy. Add eggs, a little at a time, beating well after each addition. Add 1-2tbsp flour, if necessary, to prevent mixture curdling.

★ Mix coffee with 1tsp boiling water, then beat into cake mix with chopped walnuts. Fold in the remaining flour and the baking powder with a large metal spoon.

★ Divide mixture between cupcake cases and bake for 20-25 mins until golden brown and just firm to the touch. Remove cakes from tin and leave to cool on a wire rack.

★ **TO DECORATE,** beat butter and icing sugar with a drop of boiling water until smooth and creamy. Stir in the reserved chopped walnuts, then spread icing on top of cakes and top with walnut pieces.

RECIPE, FOOD AND PROP STYLING: MITZIE WILSON PHOTO: CLIVE STREETER

Pink + white marshmallow
TOPPING

Perfect for kids, and great with a mug of hot chocolate, too

MAKES 12 **PREP** 30 MINS **BAKE** 25 MINS

RECIPE, FOOD AND PROP STYLING: MITZIE WILSON PHOTO: CLIVE BOZZARD-HILL PHOTOGRAPHY

FOR THE SPONGE
- 150g butter, at room temperature
- 150g golden caster sugar
- 3 medium eggs, beaten
- 150g self-raising flour
- ½tsp vanilla extract

FOR THE TOPPING
- 75g butter, softened
- 150g icing sugar
- Large bag of mini marshmallows

YOU WILL NEED
- A 12-hole cupcake tin, lined with paper cases

★ Preheat oven to gas mark 4/180°C (160°C in a fan oven).

★ Place butter and sugar in a mixing bowl and beat with a wooden spoon or electric whisk until butter becomes a pale colour and the mixture is light and fluffy.

★ Add eggs, a little at a time, beating well after each addition. Add 1-2tbsp flour, if necessary, to prevent the mixture curdling, then fold in the remaining flour with a large metal spoon. Stir in vanilla extract.

★ Divide mixture between cupcake cases and bake for 20-25 mins until golden brown and just firm to the touch. Remove cakes from tin and leave to cool on a wire rack.

★ **TO DECORATE,** beat butter and icing sugar together with 1-2tsp boiling water until light and creamy. Spread over cupcakes and arrange marshmallows on top.

Macaron-topped ALMOND CAKE

Decorating these cakes with mini macarons make them doubly indulgent – perfect for an afternoon tea with the girls

MAKES 12 **PREP** 20 MINS **BAKE** 25 MINS

FOR THE SPONGE
- 50g ground almonds
- 125g butter, softened
- 125g caster sugar
- 3 medium eggs, beaten
- 125g self-raising flour
- A drop of almond extract (optional)

FOR THE TOPPING
- 300ml double cream
- 12 mini macarons

YOU WILL NEED
- A 12-hole muffin tin, lined with paper cases
- A piping bag

★ Preheat oven to gas mark 4/180˚C (160˚C in a fan oven).

★ Arrange ground almonds on a baking tray and place under a hot grill for 30 seconds, then turn them over and grill until just golden and toasted. Watch carefully, as they will burn easily. Leave to cool.

★ Beat together butter and sugar in a bowl with a wooden spoon or electric whisk until really light and fluffy. Gradually add eggs, a little at a time, beating well and adding a little of the flour if the mixture begins to curdle. Beat in the flour, together with the ground almonds and almond extract, if using.

★ Divide mixture between cupcake cases and bake for 20-25 mins until golden brown and firm to the touch. Remove cakes from tin and leave to cool on a wire rack.

★ **TO DECORATE,** whip cream until it forms soft peaks, then pipe in swirls on top of cakes. Top each cake with a macaron.

RECIPE, FOOD AND PROP STYLING: MITZIE WILSON **PHOTO:** TOBY SCOTT

Know-how

Un-iced cakes will keep for up to 4 days in a cake tin. Once iced, serve within 1 hr.

Chocolate pop CANDY CAKES

Topped with a cream cheese icing, these cupcakes are not as sweet as those finished with buttercream

MAKES 12   **PREP** 35 MINS   **BAKE** 20 MINS

FOR THE SPONGE
- 50g butter
- 75g dark chocolate, chopped
- 2tbsp treacle or golden syrup
- 100g light muscovado sugar
- 50ml vegetable oil
- 100ml milk
- 2 medium eggs
- 125g self-raising flour
- 25g cocoa powder
- ½tsp bicarbonate of soda

FOR THE TOPPING
- 180g full-fat cream cheese
- 75g icing sugar
- 300ml double cream
- Chocolate popping candy (available from Squires Kitchen)

YOU WILL NEED
- A 12-hole cupcake tin, lined with paper cases
- A piping bag

★ Preheat oven to gas mark 4/180°C (160°C in a fan oven).

★ Melt butter in a small pan, then stir in chocolate until melted. Add treacle or syrup and sugar. Remove from the heat and whisk in the oil and milk until smooth, then whisk in the eggs.

★ Add flour, cocoa powder and bicarbonate of soda to the mixture and beat until evenly mixed.

★ Divide mixture between cupcake cases – they should be about two-thirds full – and bake for 20 mins until they have risen and are just firm to the touch. Remove cakes from tin and leave to cool on a wire rack.

★ **TO DECORATE,** beat cream cheese with icing sugar until smooth, then add cream and whisk until thick. Place in a piping bag, snip off the end and pipe swirls on top of the cakes. Sprinkle over the popping candy.

RECIPE, FOOD AND PROP STYLING: MITZIE WILSON PHOTO: TOBY SCOTT

Iced viola
FAIRY CAKE

These simple fairy cakes just go to show that less really is more

MAKES 12 **PREP** 30 MINS **BAKE** 25 MINS

FOR THE SPONGE
- 150g butter, at room temperature
- 150g golden caster sugar
- 3 medium eggs, beaten
- 150g self-raising flour
- ½tsp baking powder
- Zest of 1 lemon

FOR THE TOPPING
- 200g icing sugar
- 1-2tsp lemon juice
- Edible violas (finefoodspecialist.co.uk)

YOU WILL NEED
- A 12-hole cupcake tin, lined with paper cases

★ Preheat oven to gas mark 4/180°C (160°C in a fan oven).

★ Place butter and sugar in a mixing bowl and beat with a wooden spoon or electric whisk until the butter is a pale colour and the mixture is light and fluffy.

★ Add eggs, a little at a time, beating well after each addition. Add 1-2tbsp flour, if necessary, to prevent mixture curdling, then fold in the remaining flour, as well as the baking powder and lemon zest.

★ Divide mixture between cupcake cases and bake for 20-25 mins until golden brown and firm to the touch. Remove cakes from tin and leave to cool completely on a wire rack.

★ **TO DECORATE**, mix icing sugar with just enough lemon juice to make a thick pouring consistency. Spoon on top of the cakes and leave to set. Decorate with edible flowers.

RECIPE, FOOD AND PROP STYLING: MITZIE WILSON **PHOTO:** CLARE WINFIELD

Shades of PINK

These simple yet stunning cupcakes are covered with icing in a variety of pink hues. Try it with coffee and chocolate icing, too

MAKES 12 **PREP** 30 MINS **BAKE** 25 MINS

RECIPE, FOOD AND PROP STYLING: MITZIE WILSON **PHOTO:** CLIVE BOZZARD-HILL PHOTOGRAPHY

FOR THE SPONGE
- 150g butter, at room temperature
- 150g caster sugar
- 3 medium eggs, beaten
- 125g self-raising flour
- ½tsp baking powder
- 25g cocoa, sifted

FOR THE TOPPING
- 150g butter, softened
- 300g icing sugar
- ½tsp vanilla extract
- Pink food colouring

YOU WILL NEED
- A 12-hole cupcake tin, lined with paper cases
- A piping bag
- A large star nozzle

★ Preheat oven to gas mark 4/180°C (160°C in a fan oven).

★ Place butter and sugar in a bowl and beat with a wooden spoon or electric whisk until butter is a pale colour and the mixture is light and fluffy.

★ Add eggs, a little at a time, beating well after each addition. Add 1-2tbsp flour, if necessary, to prevent mixture curdling, then fold in the remaining flour and the baking powder and cocoa with a large metal spoon.

★ Divide mixture between cupcake cases and bake for 20-25 mins, until golden brown and just firm to the touch. Remove cakes from tin and leave to cool on a wire rack.

★ **TO DECORATE,** beat together butter, icing sugar, vanilla extract and a drop of boiling water in a bowl until light and creamy.

★ **TO COLOUR,** add a few drops of food colouring to give the palest shade, then remove two-thirds of icing to another bowl and add a few more drops of foods colouring. Remove half of this mixture to a third bowl and colour to a deeper shade, as desired.

★ Place palest icing in a piping bag fitted with a star-shaped nozzle and pipe a star on top of a cake, in the centre, wiggling nozzle slightly to get a frilled effect until icing covers top of cake. Repeat on remaining cakes with the other shades of icing.

Chocolate + raspberry
ROSEBUD

A drizzle of raspberry liqueur makes this a grown-up sweet

MAKES 12   **PREP** 30 MINS   **BAKE** 25 MINS

FOR THE SPONGE

- 150g butter, at room temperature
- 150g caster sugar
- 3 medium eggs, beaten
- 125g self-raising flour
- 25g cocoa powder, sifted
- ½tsp baking powder
- 2tbsp raspberry (framboise) liqueur (optional)

FOR THE TOPPING

- 150ml double cream
- 100g raspberries
- 1tsp icing sugar
- Small rosebuds or rose petals to decorate (optional)

YOU WILL NEED

- A 12-hole cupcake tin, lined with paper cases

★ Preheat oven to gas mark 4/180°C (160°C in a fan oven).

★ Place butter and sugar in a mixing bowl and beat with wooden spoon or electric whisk until butter is a pale colour and the mixture is light and fluffy.

★ Add eggs, a little at a time, beating well after each addition. Add 1-2tbsp flour, if necessary, to prevent the mixture curdling, then fold in the remaining flour and the cocoa powder and baking powder with a large metal spoon.

★ Divide mixture between cupcake cases and bake for 20-25 mins until golden brown and just firm to the touch. Leave to cool for 10 mins in tin, then spoon over liqueur, if using. Remove cakes from tin and allow to cool completely on a wire rack.

★ **TO DECORATE,** whip cream until it just holds its shape. Using a fork, squash about 10 raspberries in a small bowl and fold into the cream, then sweeten with icing sugar. Dollop on top of each cake and top with a rosebud. If you like, you could also use a knife to cut out a small circle from the centre of each cake, then fill it with a little raspberry jam and replace trimmed cake lid before decorating.

RECIPE, FOOD AND PROP STYLING: MITZIE WILSON **PHOTO:** CLIVE BOZZARD-HILL PHOTOGRAPHY

The joy of CLASSICS

Whether you're entertaining or treating your family, these tried-and-tested favourites are loved by all

Try this

These will keep, unfilled, for a couple of days in an airtight container. Recrisp in a hot oven for 1-2 mins before filling.

Tiny ECLAIRS

Fondant icing, rather than chocolate, coats these perfectly sized treats

MAKES 18-20   **PREP** 20 MINS   **BAKE** 25 MINS

FOR THE CHOUX
- 65g plain flour
- Pinch of salt
- 50g butter
- 2 medium eggs
- 300ml double cream

FOR THE ICING
- 200g fondant icing sugar
- A few drops green food colouring
- Sugar sprinkles, to decorate

YOU WILL NEED
- A large piping bag, fitted with a medium plain nozzle

★ Preheat oven to gas mark 6/200°C (180°C in a fan oven).

★ Sift flour and salt into a bowl. Place butter and 150ml cold water into a pan and bring to the boil. Now tip in the flour, all at once, and beat with a wooden spoon until the mixture forms a ball and comes away from the sides of the pan. Remove from the heat and leave to cool for a couple of mins.

★ Gradually beat eggs into flour mixture until mixture is smooth and shiny. Place choux mixture into a large piping bag fitted with a medium plain nozzle and pipe 5-6cm fingers, spaced apart, on to a baking tray. Bake for 15-18 mins until they have risen and are golden brown.

★ Remove buns from oven and make a little slit in the side of each with the point of a knife. Return to the hot oven for 5 mins to dry out. Remove and leave to cool completely.

★ **TO MAKE ICING,** mix icing sugar with enough water to give a very thick coating consistency, then add a little food colouring. Cut the choux buns in half, dip the outside of the top halves into the icing and decorate with sugar sprinkles.

★ **TO FILL** Whip cream until it just holds its shape, then pipe or spoon into the bottom half of the buns. Top with the iced half and chill until ready to serve.

RECIPE, FOOD AND PROP STYLING: MITZIE WILSON PHOTO: CLARE WINFIELD

Raspberry + almond FRIAND

This tart is a new take on the traditional cake – you could serve it as a dessert, simply warm and top with a dollop of crème fraîche

SERVES 8 **PREP** 20 MINS **BAKE** 35 MINS

FOR THE CAKE

- 125g icing sugar, plus extra for dusting
- 25g plain flour
- 175g ground almonds
- 6 medium egg whites
- 100g butter, melted
- Zest of 1 lemon
- 150g raspberries
- 25g shelled pistachios, chopped

YOU WILL NEED

- A 20cm-round (4cm deep) fluted flan tin or cake tin, greased

★ Preheat oven to gas mark 6/200°C (180°C in a fan oven).

★ Add icing sugar, flour and ground almonds to a mixing bowl and stir well.

★ Whisk egg whites in a clean, grease-free bowl until they form a thick foam. Add to almond mixture, fold together once or twice, then fold in butter and lemon zest until evenly mixed.

★ Add batter to the tin, gently spread it out, then push raspberries into mixture and scatter over pistachios.

★ **BAKE** for 30-35 mins until well risen and just firm to the touch in the centre. Allow to cool in the tin for 15 mins, then remove the sides of the tin and leave tart to cool completely. Dust with a little extra icing sugar before serving in slices.

RECIPE, FOOD AND PROP STYLING: MITZIE WILSON PHOTO: CLARE WINFIELD

Raspberry CREAM SLICES

Light-as-air sponge and tangy raspberries make these cakes irresistible

MAKES 10   **PREP** 40 MINS   **BAKE** 15 MINS

FOR THE SPONGE
- 125g caster sugar, plus extra to dust
- 3 large eggs
- 125g plain flour

FOR THE FILLING
- 3tbsp sherry (optional)
- 4tbsp raspberry jam
- 300ml double cream, whipped
- 400g raspberries
- Icing sugar, to dust

YOU WILL NEED
- A 33cm x 23cm Swiss roll tin, greased and lined with baking parchment

★ Preheat oven to gas mark 4/180°C (160°C in a fan oven).

★ Put sugar and eggs in a bowl and whisk with an electric whisk for 10 mins until pale and thick enough for the mixture to leave a trail when the whisk is lifted.

★ Sift flour into mixture and, using a large metal spoon, fold in very carefully.

★ Pour mixture into the tin and use a spatula to smooth it evenly into the corners. Bake in the centre of the oven for 10-12 mins, until it has risen and is just firm to the touch. Leave to cool completely in the tin.

★ Carefully tip cooled cake on to a board. Peel off baking parchment and cut crusts off the cake, then cut it in half lengthways to give 2 long strips.

★ Drizzle 1 strip of cake with sherry, if using, and spread with raspberry jam. Top with half the cream and arrange raspberries in rows on top. Spread over remaining cream and place second cake strip on top. Dust with icing sugar, then cut into slices.

RECIPE, FOOD AND PROP STYLING: MITZIE WILSON PHOTO: CLARE WINFIELD

Blackberry + apple
SCONE CAKE

This cake is beautifully moist thanks to the addition of blackberries and apple. Serve at teatime on a Sunday

SERVES 8 **PREP** 20 MINS **BAKE** 55 MINS

FOR THE SPONGE

- 300g self-raising flour, sifted
- 150g butter
- 100g caster sugar
- Zest of 1 orange
- 2 medium eggs, beaten
- 100ml milk
- 200g blackberries
- 1 apple
- 2tbsp demerara sugar, to decorate (optional)

YOU WILL NEED

- A 20.5cm deep, loose bottomed cake tin, greased and base lined with baking parchment

★ Preheat oven to gas mark 4/180°C (160°C in a fan oven).

★ Place flour and butter in a food processor and blend until mixture resembles fine breadcrumbs.

★ Add sugar, orange zest, eggs and milk and blend for a few seconds until just combined — but do not over mix.

★ Place half of the mixture into the tin and top with half of the blackberries. Cover with remaining cake mixture.

★ Thinly slice apples and lay on top of the mixture. Scatter over the remaining blackberries.

★ **BAKE** for 45-55 mins until cake has risen, is golden and a skewer comes out clean when inserted into the centre. Sprinkle over demerara sugar, if using. Allow to cool and serve sliced with cream, if you like. Best eaten within 2 days.

RECIPE AND FOOD STYLING: MITZIE WILSON **PROP STYLING:** SUE ROWLANDS **PHOTO:** TOBY SCOTT

Try this
With any of your favourite fruit. Raspberries, blueberries and apricots are ideal.

Try this

Rinse off the syrup glacé cherries come in, then dry them – this prevents them sinking to the bottom of the cakes.

Cherry BAKEWELLS

Delicious almond cupcakes filled with cherries – perfect with a cup of tea

MAKES 12 **PREP** 25 MINS **BAKE** 25 MINS

RECIPE, FOOD AND PROP STYLING: MITZIE WILSON PHOTO: CLIVE BOZZARD-HILL

FOR THE SPONGE
- 150g butter, at room temperature
- 150g golden caster sugar
- 3 medium eggs, beaten
- 150g self-raising flour
- 25g ground almonds
- ½tsp almond extract
- 50g glacé cherries (or dried cherries), chopped

FOR THE TOPPING
- 150g fondant icing sugar
- 6 glacé cherries, halved

YOU WILL NEED
- A 12-hole cupcake tin, lined with paper cases

★ Preheat oven to gas mark 4/180°C (160°C in a fan oven).

★ Place butter and sugar in a mixing bowl and beat with a wooden spoon or electric whisk until butter is pale and mixture is light and fluffy.

★ Add eggs, a little at a time, beating well after each addition. Add 1-2 tbsp flour, if necessary, to prevent mixture curdling then fold in remaining flour, and ground almonds, almond extract and cherries with a large metal spoon.

★ Divide mixture between cupcake cases and bake for 20-25 mins until golden brown and just firm to the touch. Remove cakes from tin and allow to cool completely on a wire rack.

★ Sift fondant icing sugar into a small bowl and add just enough water, a drop at a time, to make an icing that has a very thick pouring consistency. Spoon a little on top of each cupcake and top with half a glacé cherry.

Hot cross bun
LOAF

*While this is a popular Easter staple, you can enjoy it any time.
Try it toasted for breakfast the day after making*

MAKES 1 LOAF **PREP** 20 MINS, PLUS RISING **BAKE** 40 MINS

FOR THE LOAF
- 500g strong white bread flour
- 50g butter
- 50g golden caster sugar
- 7g sachet easy bake yeast
- ½tsp salt
- 1tsp mixed spice
- 1tsp ground cinnamon
- 250g pack Jumbo Raisins & Cranberries (available from Sainsbury's)
- 1 medium egg, beaten
- 125ml milk
- 125ml boiling water

FOR THE CROSSES
- 3tbsp plain flour

YOU WILL NEED
- A 1kg loaf tin, greased
- A small plastic piping bag

★ Preheat oven to gas mark 6/200°C (180°C in a fan oven).

★ Place flour and butter in a mixing bowl. Using your hands, rub butter into flour, then add all the other loaf ingredients. First mix to a soft dough by hand, then mix with a dough hook in an electric mixer for 5 mins, or turn on to a work surface dusted with flour and knead for 10 mins until smooth and elastic.

★ Divide dough into 8 equal pieces and roll each into a ball. Arrange them in the loaf tin and cover with oiled cling film. Leave in a warm, dry place to rise for about 45 mins to 1 hr (until just above the top of the tin).

★ Just before baking, make the crosses by mixing the plain flour with a little cold water to form a smooth, thick paste. Place in a piping bag, snip off the end and pipe crosses over the buns.

★ Bake for 30 mins, then cover with foil to prevent further browning and bake for another 10 mins. To test if the loaf is cooked, remove from tin and tap the bottom – it should sound hollow. Allow to cool completely, then slice and serve with butter.

RECIPE, FOOD AND PROP STYLING: MITZIE WILSON **PHOTO:** TOBY SCOTT

Try this
You can bake these as individual buns, if you prefer. Reduce baking time to 20-25 mins.

Try this

Instead of lemon curd, use orange curd, or swap the curd and icing for cream and berries or your favourite jam.

Vanilla sponge with
LEMON CURD

A wonderfully light summer cake, oozing with a buttery and citrussy filling

SERVES 12 **PREP** 20 MINS **BAKE** 30 MINS

FOR THE SPONGE
- 4 medium eggs, lightly beaten
- 150g caster sugar
- 1tsp vanilla extract
- 150g self-raising flour

FOR THE FILLING
- 50g butter
- 125g icing sugar, sifted, plus extra for dusting
- 2-3tbsp lemon curd

YOU WILL NEED
- 2 x 21cm round, loose bottom cake tins

★ Preheat oven to gas mark 4/180°C (160°C in a fan oven).

★ Add eggs and sugar to the bowl of a food processor and whisk until really creamy (about 5 mins).

★ Stir in vanilla extract, then slowly fold in flour, a little at a time, until it's all incorporated. Pour mixture into tins and bake for 20-30 mins until it's a pale golden colour and springy to the touch.

★ Remove from oven and leave to cool in tin for about 10 mins, then loosen edges with a knife and turn out on to a wire rack and leave to cool completely.

★ **TO MAKE FILLING,** beat butter until smooth, then add icing sugar, a little at a time, and a few drops of water. Beat until creamy, adding more or less icing sugar, as needed. Spread over 1 cake, and spread lemon curd over the other cake, then sandwich cakes together and dust with icing sugar.

RECIPE, FOOD AND PROP STYLING: HEATHER WHINNEY PHOTO: JON WHITAKER

Lemon TARTLETS

Dainty mini versions of the traditional sweet and sharp favourite

MAKES 12 PREP 30 MINS, PLUS CHILLING BAKE 20 MINS

FOR THE TARTLETS
- 175g ready-made sweet dessert shortcrust pastry
- A little flour, for dusting
- 2tbsp lemon juice
- 1 medium egg
- 2tbsp double cream
- 40g caster sugar

FOR THE TOPPING
- 1tbsp lemon curd (optional)
- A few raspberries, blueberries and redcurrants
- A few mint leaves

YOU WILL NEED
- A 5cm round cutter
- A mini tartlet tin
- Baking beans
- Baking parchment

★ Preheat oven to gas mark 6/200°C (180°C in a fan oven).

★ Roll out pastry thinly on a lightly floured work surface. Cut out circles, using the pastry cutter, and press into tins, using a ball of dough to push down evenly. Prick the base of each with a fork and chill for 10 mins to help prevent shrinkage.

★ Bake pastry cases for 5 mins, then remove from oven, prick pastry again to burst air bubbles, and return to the oven for another 4-5 mins or until they are golden brown at the edges. Remove from oven and turn down heat to gas mark 5/190°C (170°C in a fan oven).

★ In a jug, beat together lemon juice, egg, cream and sugar, then pour into tartlet cases and bake for 6-7 mins or until mixture is just set. Allow to cool.

★ **TO DECORATE,** top with a thin layer of lemon curd, if you like, and decorate with the berries and mint leaves.

RECIPE, FOOD AND PROP STYLING: MITZIE WILSON PHOTO: CLARE WINFIELD

Try this

You don't have to use lemon curd, but as the filling shrinks slightly, it gives a neater finish.

Try this

To make curls, spread
melted chocolate on to
marble, leave to cool,
then shave with a knife.

Extra special ginger
SPONGE

This eye-catching cake is studded with crystallised ginger, then filled with buttercream and topped with dark chocolate – divine!

SERVES 8 **PREP** 30 MINS **BAKE** 30 MINS

RECIPE AND FOOD STYLING: MITZIE WILSON **PROP STYLING:** SUE ROWLANDS **PHOTO:** TOBY SCOTT

FOR THE SPONGE
- 250g butter, softened
- 250g light muscovado sugar
- 5 medium eggs, beaten
- 250g self-raising flour
- 2tbsp treacle
- ½tsp baking powder
- 1tbsp ground ginger
- 50g crystallised ginger

FOR THE FILLING
- 150g butter
- 300g golden icing sugar
- Crystallised ginger and chocolate curls, to decorate

YOU WILL NEED
- 2 x 20.5cm round sponge tins, greased and lined with baking parchment

★ Preheat oven to gas mark 4/180°C (160°C in a fan oven).

★ Place butter and sugar in a mixing bowl and beat until really light and fluffy. Gradually beat in eggs, a little at a time, adding a little flour if the mixture begins to curdle. Add treacle, then fold in the rest of the flour, as well as the baking powder, ground ginger and crystallised ginger until evenly mixed.

★ Divide mixture between tins and bake for 25-30 mins until just firm in the centre. Leave to cool in tins for 5 mins, then turn out and leave to cool completely on a wire rack.

★ **TO MAKE FILLING,** beat butter and icing sugar until smooth and creamy. Use half to sandwich cakes together and pile the rest on top of the cake. Decorate with crystallised ginger and chocolate curls.

Coconut CAKE

Bring a taste of the exotic to your table with this no-fuss loaf

SERVES 12 **PREP** 15 MINS **BAKE** 45 MINS

FOR THE SPONGE

- **175g self-raising flour**
- **1tsp baking powder**
- **175g golden caster sugar**
- **50g tenderised sweetened coconut**
- **3 medium eggs**
- **150ml natural yoghurt**
- **Zest and juice of 2 limes**
- **175g butter, melted**

TO DECORATE

- 1 lime
- 125g golden icing sugar
- 1tbsp tenderised sweetened coconut

YOU WILL NEED

- 900g loaf tin, greased and lined with baking parchment

★ Preheat oven to gas mark 4/180˚C (160˚C in a fan oven).

★ Put flour, baking powder, caster sugar and coconut into a food processor and pulse to combine.

★ Break eggs into a jug with the yoghurt, lime zest and juice and mix together with a fork. Pour into dry ingredients with butter and pulse until mixture is just combined.

★ Pour mixture into loaf tin and bake for 45 mins until golden. Leave to cool for 10 mins.

★ **TO DECORATE,** peel the lime and put the flesh into a mini processor. Whizz until lump free, then add icing sugar and blend to make a smooth icing. Pour over cake and sprinkle over coconut.

RECIPE, FOOD AND PROP STYLING: FELICITY BARNUM-BOBB **PHOTO:** STEVE BAXTER

Apple + cinnamon MINI SCONES

Fresh fruit and spice make these scones extra special

MAKES 18-20 **PREP** 20 MINS **BAKE** 10 MINS

FOR THE SCONE

- 1 apple
- 250g self-raising flour, plus extra for dusting
- 1tsp baking powder
- ½tsp ground cinnamon
- 40g butter
- 25g caster sugar
- 1 medium egg
- 100ml milk
- 2tsp demerara sugar

TO SERVE

- Clotted cream
- Jam

YOU WILL NEED

- A 4cm round cutter
- A baking tray

★ Preheat oven to gas mark 7/220°C (200°C in a fan oven).

★ Peel and coarsely grate the apple. Place flour, baking powder and cinnamon in a mixing bowl. Add butter and rub it in with your fingertips until mixture resembles breadcrumbs. Stir in caster sugar and apple.

★ Beat together egg and milk. Reserve 2tbsp of mixture, then stir the remainder into the scone mix to make a soft dough. Gather dough together and turn out on to a lightly floured work surface.

★ Roll out dough until about 2cm thick, then cut out scones with a cutter. Re-roll trimmings and repeat process until all the dough has been used.

★ Place scones on baking tray and brush tops with the remaining egg and milk mixture, then sprinkle over demerara sugar.

★ Bake scones for 8-10 mins until they are golden brown and have risen. Leave to cool. Serve them with cream and jam.

RECIPE, FOOD AND PROP STYLING: MITZIE WILSON **PHOTO:** CLARE WINFIELD

Fondant FANCIES

Pretty pastel treats look gorgeous, and taste it too!

MAKES 20 **PREP** 1 HR, PLUS CHILLING **BAKE** 40 MINS

FOR THE SPONGE
- 250g butter, softened
- 250g caster sugar
- 5 medium eggs, beaten
- 1tsp vanilla extract
- 250g self-raising flour

FOR THE TOPPING
- 125g butter
- 200g icing sugar, plus extra for dusting
- 3tbsp apricot jam
- 250g marzipan
- 750g fondant icing sugar
- Pink, orange and green food colourings

YOU WILL NEED
- A 20cm-square cake tin, greased and lined with baking parchment
- Small plastic piping bags

★ Preheat oven to gas mark 4/180°C (160°C in a fan oven).

★ Place butter and sugar in a mixing bowl and beat until really light and creamy. Gradually beat in eggs, a little at a time, and vanilla extract. Fold in flour until mixed, then add to cake tin and spread it out evenly.

★ Bake for 35-40 mins until golden brown, firm to the touch and just shrinking away from the sides of the tin. Allow to cool in tin for 10 mins. Turn upside down and leave to cool on a wire rack.

★ **TO MAKE TOPPING,** beat together butter and icing sugar with a drop of boiling water to give a smooth, spreadable icing.

★ When cake is cold, turn it upside down and spread the top with jam.

★ Dust a worktop with icing sugar and, very thinly, roll out marzipan. Place on top of the cake and trim it to fit.

★ Cut cake into 4cm strips and cut each strip into 4cm squares (you will now have 20 small cakes).

★ Cover 4 sides of each little cake (but not the tops) with buttercream. Do this as neatly as you can, as it will help the fondant icing look smooth when poured over. Chill cakes for 30 mins.

★ **TO MAKE ICING,** sieve fondant icing sugar into a bowl and add just enough water to give a very thick pouring consistency. Divide icing into 3 bowls and add 1 food colouring to each.

★ To coat cakes, pour a little fondant icing over each, spreading it down the sides, and leave to set on a wire rack or board.

★ Place remaining icing in 3 different piping bags, snip off the ends and drizzle icing, in contrasting colours, over cakes.

RECIPE, FOOD AND PROP STYLING: MITZIE WILSON PHOTO: KATIE WILSON

Try this

The cakes are easier to cut and coat if the sponge is made a day in advance.

Try this

Make this extra special and for adults only by adding a little orange liqueur to the ganache.

Tunis CAKE

This Madeira-style bake was popular in the 1960s and is now enjoying a revival

SERVES 10 **PREP** 45 MINS, PLUS SETTING **BAKE** 1 HR 30 MINS

RECIPE AND FOOD STYLING: MITZIE WILSON **PROP STYLING:** SUE ROWLANDS **PHOTO:** TOBY SCOTT

FOR THE SPONGE

- 225g butter, softened
- 300g caster sugar
- 4 medium eggs
- 275g plain flour
- 2½tsp baking powder
- 75g ground almonds
- Zest and juice of 1 orange

FOR THE GANACHE

- 300ml double cream
- 300g plain chocolate, broken into small pieces

FOR THE CANDIED ZEST

- 1 orange
- 50g caster sugar

YOU WILL NEED

- A 20.5cm round, deep cake tin, greased and lined with baking parchment to the top of the tin

★ Preheat oven to gas mark 3/170°C (150°C in a fan oven).

★ Place butter and sugar in a mixing bowl and beat with a wooden spoon or electric mixer until light and fluffy. Gradually beat in eggs, one at a time, until smooth, adding a little flour if the mixture starts to curdle.

★ Fold in remaining flour, plus baking powder, ground almonds and orange zest and juice. Add mixture to cake tin and bake for 1 hr 30 mins, or until cake feels firm in the centre and a skewer comes out clean when inserted in the centre. Remove cake from tin, but don't remove baking parchment, and leave to cool. When cool, return cake to cake tin.

★ **TO MAKE GANACHE,** bring cream to the boil, then remove from the heat. Add chocolate, leave for 2 mins until melted, then whisk until smooth. Pour ganache over cake and leave to set for at least 4 hrs.

★ **TO MAKE CANDIED ZEST,** pare orange peel with a potato peeler, then cut into long strips. Place in a small pan with 4tbsp boiling water and half of the caster sugar and boil for 1 min. Drain, pat dry on kitchen paper, then roll zest in remaining sugar. Dry in the residual heat of the oven for about 1 hr, or on a radiator overnight (when dry, they will keep in a container for 1 week). Arrange candied zest on top of the ganache around the outside edge of the cake.

Lemon drizzle BARS

The secret ingredient here is the ground almonds, which keeps the sponge wonderfully moist. All it needs is a cup of tea

MAKES 18 **PREP** 15 MINS **BAKE** 30 MINS

FOR THE BARS

- 200g butter, softened
- 350g golden caster sugar
- 4 medium eggs
- 3 lemons
- 100g pack ground almonds
- 150g self-raising flour, sifted

YOU WILL NEED

- A 20.5cm x 30.5cm rectangular tin, lined with greaseproof paper

★ Preheat oven to gas mark 4/180°C (160°C in a fan oven).

★ Cream together butter and 200g of the caster sugar until pale and fluffy. Whisk in eggs, one at a time, followed by zest of 3 lemons.

★ Whisk ground almonds and flour into lemon mixture until smooth. Pour into tin and bake for 25-30 mins until it has risen and is firm — when a skewer inserted into the centre of it comes out clean, it is ready.

★ **FOR THE LEMON DRIZZLE** Mix together remaining sugar and juice of 2 lemons. Remove cake from oven and pour over lemon drizzle while still hot. Leave to cool, then cut into 18 bars.

RECIPE AND FOOD STYLING: KATY GREENWOOD **PROP STYLING:** FELICITY BARNUM-BOBB **PHOTO:** ROB WHITE

Try this

If you prefer not to use nuts, you can replace the almonds with polenta or cornmeal, which give a similar texture.

Know-how

As with any sponge cake, don't open the oven door too early or your cake may sink in the middle.

Coffee + walnut SPONGE

An easy cake that tastes just like the ones you had in childhood or at the village fete. The key is to be generous with the coffee flavouring and walnuts

MAKES 18-20 **PREP** 20 MINS **BAKE** 25 MINS

FOR THE SPONGE

- 175g butter, at room temperature
- 175g caster sugar
- 3 medium eggs, lightly beaten
- 175g self-raising flour, sifted
- 3tsp instant coffee, mixed with 1tbsp boiling water
- 75g walnut halves, roughly chopped, plus a handful for topping (leave as halves)

FOR THE ICING

- 175 butter, at room temperature
- 375g icing sugar, sifted
- 3tsp instant coffee, mixed with 1tbsp boiling water

YOU WILL NEED

- 2 x 20.5cm loose-bottom cake tins, greased and base lined with greaseproof paper

★ Preheat oven to gas mark 4/180°C (160°C in a fan oven).

★ In a large bowl or food processor, add butter and sugar and beat with a whisk or electric beater until pale and light. Add eggs, a little at a time, and continue beating, tipping in a little flour as you go to stop it from curdling. When combined, add remaining flour and, using a metal spoon, fold into mixture, taking care not to knock air out of mix. Gently stir in coffee mixture and chopped walnuts — it should be a dropping consistency.

★ Divide mixture between tins, making sure tops are level and smooth, then bake for 20-25 mins till golden. To check if cake is cooked, insert a skewer into the centre — it should come out clean. If not, cook a little longer. Remove cake from oven and leave to cool.

★ **TO MAKE ICING,** beat butter with an electric beater until soft, then add icing sugar and beat until smooth. Add coffee mixture and stir — if it's too stiff, add a little more water and, if it's too wet, add a little more icing sugar.

★ Once cakes are cool, slide a knife around edges of tin and remove cakes. Sit 1 cake on a plate and spread with half of the icing, then top with other cake and smother top with remaining icing. Decorate with walnut halves. This cake is best eaten within a couple of days.

RECIPE, FOOD, PROP STYLING: HEATHER WHINNEY PHOTO: WILLIAM SHAW

Stripy rock RED VELVET

Quick and easy to make, these will brighten up any table

MAKES 6 **PREP** 25 MINS **BAKE** 20 MINS

FOR THE SPONGE
- 150ml buttermilk
- 250ml sunflower oil
- 1tsp concentrated red food colouring
- 2 medium eggs
- 225g caster sugar
- 1tsp vanilla extract
- 225g plain flour
- 2tbsp cocoa powder
- 2tsp bicarbonate of soda
- 2tsp vinegar

FOR THE ICING
- 50g butter
- 50g icing sugar
- 150g cream cheese
- 1 stick of stripy rock, roughly chopped

YOU WILL NEED
- 12-hole mini sandwich tin, greased

★ Preheat oven to gas mark 4/180°C (160°C in a fan oven).

★ Mix together buttermilk, oil and food colouring, then place in a mixing bowl and add remaining sponge ingredients. Beat well with a wooden spoon until smooth, then divide mixture between the cake tin.

★ Bake for 18-20 mins until just firm to the touch. Leave to cool in tin for 10 mins, then turn out and leave to cool completely.

★ **TO MAKE ICING,** beat butter and icing sugar until smooth, then beat in cream cheese. Use to sandwich the cakes together in pairs and spread a little on top of each. Top with candy canes.

★ These will keep in the fridge for 3 days.

RECIPE, FOOD AND PROP STYLING: MITZIE WILSON **PHOTO:** CLARE WINFIELD

Lemon + honey
BUNDT

Give your coffee break an upgrade with this stunning but simple cake

SERVES 12 **PREP** 15 MINS **BAKE** 45 MINS

FOR THE CAKE
- 150g butter, melted and left to cool
- 150g caster sugar
- 150g runny honey
- 2 medium eggs
- 150ml sour cream
- 300g self-raising flour
- Juice and zest of ½ lemon

FOR THE TOPPING
- 1 lemon
- 50g granulated sugar
- 200g fondant icing sugar

YOU WILL NEED
- A 1.25 litre Bundt tin, greased and dusted with flour

★ Preheat oven to gas mark 4/180°C (160°C in a fan oven).

★ Place all cake ingredients into a bowl and beat until smooth. Add to cake tin, spread out and bake for 40-45 mins or until golden and firm and a skewer comes out clean when inserted in the centre. Leave to cool for 10 mins – don't worry if it sinks a little – then turn out and leave to cool completely on a wire rack.

★ **TO MAKE CANDIED PEEL** Using a potato peeler, pare lemon rind and cut into thin strips. Place in a small pan with 100ml water and 25g of the granulated sugar. Boil for 5 mins, then drain and dry on kitchen paper. Toss in the remaining sugar, place on a baking tray and leave to dry in the residual heat of the oven for 1 hr, or on a hot radiator until it is dried.

★ **TO MAKE THE ICING,** squeeze juice from pared lemon and add enough to fondant icing sugar to make a thick pouring icing. Drizzle over the cake and decorate with candied lemon.

★ The cake will keep for 1 week in a cake tin.

RECIPE, FOOD AND PROP STYLING: MITZIE WILSON **PHOTO:** TOBY SCOTT

Daisy SWISS ROLL

*Pre-baked decorations give this pale sponge
a colourful floral look*

SERVES 8 PREP 30 MINS, PLUS COOLING BAKE 15 MINS

FOR THE SPONGE
- 4 medium eggs, separated
- 165g caster sugar
- ½tsp vanilla extract
- 125g self-raising flour
- Pink and blue gel food colourings (such as Dr Oetker)

FOR THE FILLING
- 50g butter, softened
- 100g icing sugar
- 2tbsp raspberry jam

YOU WILL NEED
- A 25cm x 38cm Swiss roll tin, lined with 2 layers of baking parchment (to prevent browning)
- Baking parchment
- Piping bags

★ Preheat oven to gas mark 4/180°C (160°C in a fan oven).

★ Place egg whites in a large, clean mixing bowl and whisk until they form stiff peaks. Gradually whisk in 65g of the caster sugar until smooth and glossy.

★ In a second bowl, whisk egg yolks, vanilla extract and remaining 100g caster sugar until pale and thick. Sift over flour, then add meringue mix. Using a large metal spoon, fold together until evenly combined, but take care not to knock out all of the air.

★ Place 3tbsp of the mixture into a small bowl and add a little pink food colouring. Place in a piping bag and snip off the end, then pipe daisy shapes over the base of the tin. Place 1tbsp of mixture in a second bowl and mix in a little blue food colouring. Place in a piping bag and pipe a few blue dots in-between the daisies.

★ Bake shapes for 2 mins, then remove from the oven and carefully spread the remaining uncoloured cake mixture over the top. Return to the oven and bake for 10-12 mins until sponge is a pale golden colour and is just firm to the touch.

★ Place a sheet of baking parchment on a work surface and tip sponge out on to it, then gently peel off layers of baking parchment.

★ Score a line 3cm in from one short edge. Then, using the paper to help you, tightly roll up Swiss roll (along with the paper) from this end. Leave to cool for about 30 mins while you make the filling.

★ **TO MAKE THE FILLING** Beat butter, icing sugar and jam together. Carefully unroll sponge once cool, remove baking parchment and spread over the filling. Carefully re-roll Swiss roll. This is best served on the day it is made.

RECIPE, FOOD AND PROP STYLING: MITZIE WILSON PHOTO: TOBY SCOTT

Peanut butter CHEESECAKE

This no-bake recipe is very easy to make and will disappear in seconds as it's not too sweet or too rich, but very delicious

SERVES 8-10 **PREP** 30 MINS, PLUS CHILLING **BAKE** NONE

FOR THE BASE

- 300g double chocolate digestive biscuits
- 50g butter
- 3 leaves of gelatine
- 600g cream cheese
- 200g crunchy peanut butter
- 100g caramel sauce or caramel condensed milk

FOR THE TOPPING

- 150ml double cream
- 25g dark chocolate, melted
- 50g honey roasted peanuts

YOU WILL NEED

- A 18cm round springform cake tin

★ Roughly break up biscuits and pulse in a food processor to make fine crumbs. Melt butter in a medium pan, then add biscuit crumbs and stir well, heating gently for 1 min more. Tip mixture into cake tin, press down well and chill for 30 mins.

★ Soak gelatine in 4tbsp cold water for 10 mins. Meanwhile, beat together cream cheese, peanut butter and caramel until evenly mixed. Warm gelatine and water in a small pan until dissolved, but do not boil. Leave to cool for 5-10 mins.

★ Gradually pour gelatine into cream-cheese mixture, whisking well until combined. Spread evenly over biscuit base and chill for at least 2 hours.

★ **TO MAKE TOPPING,** whip cream until thick, then spoon over cheesecake. Drizzle with melted chocolate and scatter over peanuts.

RECIPE, FOOD AND PROP STYLING: MITZIE WILSON **PHOTO:** TOBY SCOTT

The joy of
CHOCOLATE

Enjoy this favourite treat in every mouth-watering form possible
– torte, cakes, roulades, flapjacks and more!

Try this

Natural raspberry extract, which is used in the pink heart, can also be used in meringues, sauces or ice cream.

Hidden heart CAKE

The raspberry-flavoured heart, which can only be seen when you slice the cake, perfectly complements the chocolate flavours

SERVES 12   **PREP** 30 MINS   **BAKE** 1 HR 40 MINS

RECIPE, FOOD AND PROP STYLING: MITZIE WILSON PHOTO: TOBY SCOTT

FOR THE PINK HEART
- 25g butter, softened
- 125g caster sugar
- 2 medium eggs, beaten
- 125g self-raising flour
- 1tsp raspberry extract (available from Lakeland, optional)
- A little pink food colouring

FOR THE CHOCOLATE CAKE
- 175g butter, softened
- 175g caster sugar
- 3 medium eggs, beaten
- 150g self-raising flour
- 25g cocoa powder, sifted

TO DECORATE
- 100ml double cream
- 200g milk chocolate, finely chopped
- 100g raspberries

YOU WILL NEED
- 450g and 900g loaf tins, both greased and lined with baking parchment
- Heart-shaped cutter (about 6cm)

★ Preheat oven to gas mark 4/180°C (160°C in a fan oven).

★ **TO MAKE THE HEART,** beat butter and sugar together until really light and fluffy. Gradually add eggs, a little at a time, beating well and adding a little flour if the mixture begins to curdle. Beat in remaining flour, the raspberry extract, if using, and add food colouring to give the desired shade.

★ Place mixture in smaller loaf tin and bake for about 45 mins or until cake is firm in the centre and a skewer comes out clean when inserted in the centre. Allow to cool for 10 mins, then turn out cake and leave to cool completely. Slice cake thickly and, using the cutter, cut a heart shape out of each slice.

★ **TO MAKE THE CHOCOLATE CAKE,** beat butter and sugar together until really light and fluffy. Gradually add eggs, a little at a time, beating well and adding a little flour if the mixture begins to curdle. Beat in remaining flour and the cocoa powder. Place half of the mixture in larger cake tin, then arrange heart-shaped cake slices close together on top of cake mixture, with the pointed ends facing down.

★ Spread over remaining cake mixture and bake for 50-55 mins until firm to the touch. Allow to cool for 10 mins, then turn out on a wire rack and leave to cool completely.

★ **TO DECORATE CAKE,** heat cream until it just comes to the boil. Add chocolate, leave until melted, then stir until smooth. Chill until thick, then spread over cake. Top with raspberries.

★ The cake will keep for 4 days, without the raspberries, in a cake tin.

Chocolate + cranberry FLAPJACKS

Keep these in a biscuit tin, so they're on hand when a sweet craving hits

MAKES 16 **PREP** 15 MINS **BAKE** 35 MINS

FOR THE FLAPJACKS

- 150g butter
- 50g plain chocolate
- 2tbsp cocoa powder
- 225g demerara sugar
- 75g golden syrup
- 300g porridge oats
- 100g dried or glacé cherries or dried cranberries

YOU WILL NEED

- A 15cm x 28cm tray bake tin, lined with baking parchment

★ Preheat oven to gas mark 3/170°C (150°C in a fan oven).

★ Melt butter in a medium pan and add chocolate, cocoa powder, sugar and syrup. Stir until chocolate has melted.

★ Stir in oats and cherries or cranberries, mixing well.

★ Add mixture to a tray bake tin and press flat with damp hands.

★ Bake for 30-35 mins. Remove from oven and leave to cool completely in tin. When cold, remove from tin and cut into bars.

★ These flapjacks will keep for up to 2 weeks in a cake tin.

RECIPE, FOOD AND PROP STYLING: MITZIE WILSON **PHOTO:** TOBY SCOTT

Try this

You can bake the cake in 2 sandwich tins if you prefer — but cook them for less time, just 20-30 mins.

Chocolate finger FUDGE CAKE

This is a wonderfully rich cake – perfect for a celebratory get-together

SERVES 12 PREP 20 MINS BAKE 1 HR

RECIPE, FOOD AND PROP STYLING: MITZIE WILSON **PHOTO:** TOBY SCOTT

FOR THE SPONGE
- 100g plain chocolate
- 100g butter, softened
- 250ml milk
- 1tbsp wine vinegar
- 1tbsp cocoa powder, sifted
- 300g self-raising flour, sifted
- 1tsp bicarbonate of soda, sifted
- 225g golden caster sugar
- 2 eggs

FOR THE GANACHE
- 225g plain chocolate, broken into pieces
- 100g butter
- 142ml carton double cream
- 2 packs chocolate finger biscuits
- An assortment of chocolate buttons

YOU WILL NEED
- A 20cm round, deep cake tin, greased and lined with baking parchment

★ Preheat oven to gas mark 4/180°C (160°C in a fan oven). Place chocolate and 50g of butter in a bowl and melt over a pan of simmering water. Remove from the heat and stir in remaining butter.

★ Mix together milk and vinegar in a jug. Place all the other cake ingredients in a mixing bowl, then pour in milk mixture and chocolate mixture. Beat until smooth. Add to cake tin and bake for 1 hr until firm in the centre. Leave to cool in tin for 10 mins, then turn out on to a wire rack to cool completely.

★ Meanwhile, make chocolate ganache. Melt chocolate and butter together in the microwave for 3 mins on medium, stirring halfway through. Alternatively, melt chocolate and butter in a bowl over a pan of just simmering water. Stir until smooth, then beat in cream. Leave to cool slightly.

★ Cut cake in half horizontally and spread a little ganache over one half, then sandwich cakes together. Spread remaining ganache over the top and sides of cake.

★ Place chocolate fingers around the outside of the cake, and arrange chocolate buttons in flower shapes on the top.

★ This will keep for up to 1 week in a cake tin.

Chocolate tarts with
BLACKBERRIES

This makes an impressive dinner party dessert with a drizzle of cream

MAKES 12 **PREP** 20 MINS, PLUS SETTING **BAKE** 20 MINS

FOR THE PASTRY
- 75g icing sugar
- 150g plain flour, plus extra for dusting
- 25g cocoa powder
- 100g butter, cut into cubes
- 1 medium egg yolk
- 1 tbsp cold milk

FOR THE FILLING
- 6tbsp blackberry jam
- 300ml double cream
- 2tbsp runny honey or golden syrup
- 200g plain chocolate
- 100g butter

TO DECORATE
- 200g blackberries
- A little edible gold leaf
- A few mint leaves

YOU WILL NEED
- 12 x 8cm individual tart tins or 7cm brioche tins
- Baking parchment
- Baking beans

★ Preheat oven to gas mark 4/180°C (160°C in a fan oven).

★ **TO MAKE PASTRY,** add icing sugar, flour and cocoa powder to a food processor. Add butter and pulse until mixture resembles fine breadcrumbs (or place in a bowl and rub butter in with your fingertips until mixture resembles breadcrumbs). Add egg yolk and milk, then mix again until just combined. Turn out on a lightly floured work surface and gather dough into a ball. Wrap in cling film and chill.

★ Cut pastry into 12 equal pieces and roll out each on a lightly floured surface so it is large enough to line a tart tin. Line pastry with circles of baking parchment (snip the edges so the paper fits better) and fill with baking beans. Bake for 15 mins.

★ Carefully remove baking beans and baking parchment and return tart cases to the oven for 5 mins.

★ **FOR THE FILLING,** spoon a little jam into each tart and leave to cool. Place cream and honey in a pan and bring to the boil. Remove from the heat, add chocolate and stir until melted. Add butter and stir until smooth. Leave to cool a little, then pour mixture into pastry cases and leave to set in the fridge.

★ **TO DECORATE** Roll blackberries in gold leaf and arrange a few on top of each tart, along with a mint leaf.

★ These will keep for up to 3 days in the fridge.

RECIPE, FOOD AND PROP STYLING: MITZIE WILSON PHOTO: TOBY SCOTT

Stripy raspberry GATEAU

Everyone will wonder how you get the stripes inside this gorgeous cake topped with summer berries – but it's easier than you think

SERVES 10 **PREP** 1 HR **BAKE** 15 MINS

RECIPE, FOOD AND PROP STYLING: MITZIE WILSON PHOTO: TOBY SCOTT

FOR THE SPONGE
- 6 medium eggs
- 200g caster sugar
- 100g plain flour
- 40g cocoa powder

FOR THE FILLING
- 6tbsp raspberry jam
- 300ml double cream

TO DECORATE
- 125ml double cream
- 200g plain chocolate, finely chopped
- 200g raspberries

YOU WILL NEED
- A 23cm x 33cm Swiss roll tin, lined with baking parchment
- A 20cm round springform tin, lined with baking parchment

★ Preheat oven to gas mark 4/180°C (160°C in a fan oven).

★ Place eggs and sugar in a bowl and, using an electric whisk, beat until mixture is thick and pale and holds its shape when whisk is lifted. Whisk in 2tbsp hot water then, using a large spoon, add flour and cocoa and fold in until smooth, trying not to knock out all the air. Divide mixture between tins and place in the oven.

★ **BAKE SWISS ROLL** for 8-10 mins until just firm in the centre – remove it from the oven quickly, then close the oven door and continue to cook **ROUND CAKE** for a further 5 mins until it is also firm in the centre and has started to shrink away from the sides of the tin. Turn out both sponges and remove baking parchment. Allow to cool completely.

★ Cut round cake in half horizontally and spread cut surfaces with a little raspberry jam. Place 1 round cake on a plate.

★ Spread half of the remaining jam over the Swiss roll. Whip cream until it just holds its shape, then fold in remaining jam. Spread cream over Swiss roll, then cut lengthways into 5 equal strips. Roll up 1 strip tightly and place in centre of round cake. Wrap another strip around it, joining the edges. Continue with all the strips, joining edges as you go, so you create a large spiral (the same size as the round cake when all the strips have been added). Place other round cake, jam side down, on top. Wrap cake in cling film and chill for at least 1 hr.

★ **TO DECORATE,** heat cream in a pan, add chocolate and leave for 5 mins. Stir until smooth and glossy and allow to cool until slightly thickened, then pour over cake, spreading it over the sides. Chill until ready to serve, topped with raspberries.

White truffle
CAKE EGGS

These truffles-with-a-difference are filled with sponge cake, not chocolate

MAKES 12 **PREP** 30 MINS, PLUS CHILLING **BAKE** NONE

FOR THE BUTTERCREAM
- 50g butter, softened
- 100g icing sugar
- 350g sponge or Madeira cake

FOR THE TOPPING
- 200g good-quality white cooking chocolate
- A little pink concentrated paste food colouring
- Sugar sprinkles

YOU WILL NEED
- Small cupcake cases
- A small plastic piping bag

★ **TO MAKE BUTTERCREAM**, beat butter and icing sugar together until smooth.

★ Crumble cake into a bowl and stir in enough buttercream to bring mixture to a stiff paste. Using your hands, roll paste into small egg shapes. Place on a plate and chill until firm.

★ **TO MAKE TOPPING**, finely chop chocolate and place in a bowl over a pan of gently simmering water until melted. Reserve 2tbsp chocolate in a separate bowl and dip each cake egg into the rest of the chocolate. Shake off the excess and place in a paper case. Add a little food colouring to reserved chocolate (melt again if it has hardened), then place in a piping bag, snip off the end and drizzle over truffles. Scatter over sugar sprinkles and refrigerate truffles until ready to serve.

RECIPE, FOOD AND PROP STYLING: MITZIE WILSON **PHOTO:** CLARE WINFIELD

Chocolate toffee
POPCORN CAKE

With smooth caramel and crisp popcorn, make this the new movie night favourite

MAKES 12 **PREP** 20 MINS **BAKE** 30 MINS

FOR THE SPONGE
- 175g plain chocolate
- 200g butter
- 200g self-raising flour
- 300g light muscovado sugar
- 25g cocoa powder
- 1tsp baking powder
- 4 medium eggs

FOR THE FILLING + TOPPING
- 300ml double cream
- 4tbsp caramel condensed milk or dulce de leche
- Bag of toffee and chocolate popcorn

YOU WILL NEED
- 2 x 20.5cm round sponge tins, greased and base lined with parchment paper

★ Preheat oven to gas mark 4/180°C (160°C in a fan oven).

★ Place 100ml hot water in a small pan, add chocolate and butter and heat gently until melted, then remove from the heat.

★ Place flour, sugar, cocoa powder and baking powder in a mixing bowl. Beat in eggs, then pour in chocolate mixture, beating until smooth.

★ Divide mixture between tins and bake for 30 mins until just firm in the centre. Allow to cool for 10 mins, then turn out on a wire rack and leave to cool completely.

★ **FOR FILLING + TOPPING** Whip cream until it just holds its shape, then put 1 cake on a plate and spread over some cream. Top with caramel, add about a third of the popcorn, then place second cake on top. Spoon over more cream and scatter over remaining popcorn.

★ The cake will keep for 3 days in the fridge.

RECIPE, FOOD AND PROP STYLING: MITZIE WILSON PHOTO: TOBY SCOTT

Meringue MERVEILLEUX

*Move over cupcakes, these towers of meringues and cream
are the latest cake craze from France. Divine!*

SERVES 6 PREP 1 HR BAKE 45 MINS

FOR THE MERINGUE
- 2 medium egg whites
- 100g caster sugar
- 2tsp cocoa powder

FOR THE FILLING
- 150ml double cream
- 100g butter, diced
- 150g plain chocolate (70% cocoa solids)
- 2tbsp light muscovado sugar
- 2tbsp hazelnut or almond liqueur (optional)

TO DECORATE
- Chocolate sprinkles

YOU WILL NEED
- A 5cm biscuit cutter
- 2 sheets of baking parchment
- 2 baking trays
- 2 piping bags
- A large plain nozzle and a large star nozzle

★ Preheat oven to gas mark ½ /130°C (110°C in a fan oven).

★ Using a biscuit cutter as a guide, draw 9 circles on each sheet of baking parchment. Turn paper upside down on top of baking trays.

★ **TO MAKE MERINGUE,** whisk egg whites until they form stiff peaks, adding caster sugar, 1 tbsp at a time, until mixture is smooth, glossy and thick. Whisk in cocoa powder.

★ Place meringue in a piping bag with a large plain nozzle and pipe mixture on to circles on baking parchment to form flat discs (hold nozzle vertically, about 1cm from paper, and press until meringue fills the shape). Press down any peaks with your finger.

★ Bake for 45 mins or until meringues are crisp and you can lift them off the paper. Leave to cool completely.

★ **TO MAKE FILLING** Place all the ingredients in a small pan and heat very gently, stirring until butter and chocolate have melted and mixture is smooth. Pour into a bowl and allow to cool completely – it will set firm. Place in a mixing bowl and whisk until it is much paler.

★ Place filling in a piping bag fitted with a large star-shaped nozzle and pipe a swirl on top of 6 meringues. Arrange another meringue on top of each, then pipe another layer of filling. Place the last meringues on top of each, with the flat-side up.

★ Using a palette knife, coat sides of towers with more filling, then roll in chocolate sprinkles. If necessary, chill meringues at each stage so they're easier to handle. Finally, pipe a swirl of filling on top.

★ These will keep for up to 2 days in the fridge.

RECIPE, FOOD AND PROP STYLING: MITZIE WILSON **PHOTO:** TOBY SCOTT

Try this

To make curls, spread melted chocolate on to marble, leave to cool, then shave with a knife.

Brandied prune
MARQUISE

This make-ahead velvety dessert is perfect for stress-free entertaining

SERVES 10-12 **PREP** 40 MINS, PLUS SETTING **BAKE** NONE

FOR THE CAKE

- 100g ready-to-eat dried prunes
- 3tbsp brandy
- 75g butter
- 150g plain chocolate (70% cocoa solids), chopped
- 3 medium egg yolks
- 75g caster sugar
- 250ml double cream

TO DECORATE

- Chocolate curls (see tip, left)

YOU WILL NEED

- A 450g loaf tin, lined with baking parchment

★ Cut prunes into small pieces and place in a bowl with brandy, then leave to soak.

★ Place butter in a small pan and heat until melted. Add chocolate and leave for a few minutes to melt, then stir together until smooth.

★ Whisk egg yolks and sugar in a medium bowl until thick and pale. Place bowl over gently simmering water (don't let it touch the water) and continue to whisk until yolk mixture is just hot. Don't overheat or eggs will curdle. Remove from the heat and whisk in chocolate mixture.

★ Whisk cream until it just holds its shape, then fold into chocolate mixture with prunes and brandy.

★ Spoon mixture into prepared tin and leave to set for at least 6 hours in the fridge, then turn out, peel away baking parchment and decorate with chocolate curls. Slice to serve.

★ This can be prepared 2 days in advance and kept in the fridge.

RECIPE, FOOD AND PROP STYLING: MITZIE WILSON PHOTO: TOBY SCOTT

Mega chocolate TRAY BAKE

This large cake is perfect for when you're having a crowd round – top it with your favourite chocolates or sweets

SERVES 18 PREP 25 MINS BAKE 30 MINS

FOR THE CAKE
- 175g plain chocolate, chopped
- 200g butter, at room temperature
- 4 medium eggs, beaten
- 200g self-raising flour
- 300g light muscovado sugar
- 25g cocoa powder
- 1tsp baking powder

FOR THE ICING
- 2tbsp cocoa powder
- 50g butter
- 2tbsp golden syrup
- 300g golden icing sugar

TO DECORATE
- A few chocolates or sweets

YOU WILL NEED
- A 23cm x 30.5cm x 5cm tray bake tin, lined with baking parchment

★ Preheat oven to gas mark 4/180°C (160°C in a fan oven).

★ Place chocolate in a small pan with butter and 100ml water. Heat gently, stirring until chocolate and butter have melted. Leave to cool until mixture is cool enough for you to place your finger in it comfortably (about 5 mins). Beat in eggs, a little at a time, with a wooden spoon.

★ Mix flour, sugar, cocoa powder and baking powder together in a bowl, then beat in chocolate mixture to make a smooth batter.

★ Pour into cake tin and bake for 30 mins until firm to the touch and just shrinking away from the sides of the tin.

★ Leave to cool in tin for 10 mins, then turn out on to a wire rack and leave to cool completely.

★ **TO MAKE ICING,** place cocoa powder, butter, syrup and icing sugar into a mixing bowl and beat together until smooth, adding a little boiling water, if necessary, to give a spreading consistency. Spread on top of cake and decorate with chocolates or sweets of your choice (we used toffee popcorn and Maltesers). Cut into squares to serve.

RECIPE AND FOOD STYLING: MITZIE WILSON PROP STYLING: SUE ROWLANDS PHOTO: TOBY SCOTT

Try this

Replace the marzipan and apricots with dark chocolate and dried cherries.

Apricot, almond + white choc
LOAF

This is a fabulously crumbly, rich cake that's perfect for taking along on a picnic

SERVES 8-10 **PREP** 25 MINS **BAKE** 1 HR 10 MINS

FOR THE SPONGE
- 200g butter, softened
- 100g caster sugar
- 4 medium eggs
- 200g self-raising flour
- 200g white chocolate, roughly chopped
- 100g ready-to-eat dried apricots, roughly chopped
- 150g marzipan, cut into 1cm chunks
- 50g flaked almonds

YOU WILL NEED
- A 900g loaf tin, lined with baking parchment

★ Preheat oven to gas mark 2/150°C (130°C in fan oven).

★ Beat together butter and sugar until light and creamy, then gradually beat in eggs, adding a little flour if the mixture curdles. Add remaining flour and the chocolate, apricots, marzipan and most of the flaked almonds.

★ Spoon mixture into loaf tin, spreading it evenly, then sprinkle over remaining almonds. Bake for 1 hr-1 hr 10 mins or until firm in the centre and golden brown.

★ Allow to cool in tin for 20 mins, then turn out on to a wire rack and leave to cool completely. Slice to serve.

RECIPE, FOOD AND PROP STYLING: MITZIE WILSON **PHOTO**: TOBY SCOTT

Chocolate ECLAIRS

This classic dessert is given an update with hazelnut-flavoured cream – light and delicious

MAKES 9 PREP 20 MINS BAKE 25 MINS

FOR THE CHOUX
- 65g plain flour
- A pinch of salt
- 50g butter
- 2 eggs

FOR THE ICING
- 1tbsp cocoa powder
- 200g fondant icing sugar
- Edible gold glitter stars (optional)

FOR THE FILLING
- 300ml double cream
- 3tbsp chocolate hazelnut spread (we used Nutella)

YOU WILL NEED
- A large piping bag and a medium plain nozzle

★ Preheat oven to gas mark 6/200°C (180°C in a fan oven).

★ Sift flour and salt into a bowl. Place butter and 150ml cold water into a pan and bring to the boil. Tip in flour, all at once, and beat well with a wooden spoon until mixture forms a ball and comes away from the sides of the pan. Remove from the heat and leave to cool for a few mins.

★ Gradually beat eggs into flour mixture, beating until it is smooth, thick and shiny, then add to a piping bag, fitted with a medium plain nozzle.

★ Pipe mixture on to baking tray in 10cm lengths. Bake for 15-18 mins until they have risen and are golden brown. Remove choux buns from oven and make a little slit in the side of each with the point of a knife. Return to the hot oven for 5 mins to dry out, then remove and leave to cool completely.

★ **TO MAKE ICING,** mix cocoa powder with 1tbsp boiling water to make a paste, then mix with icing sugar to give a very thick coating consistency, adding extra water, if needed. Cut eclairs in half and dip the outside of the top halves into the icing. Sprinkle with gold stars.

★ **TO MAKE FILLING,** whip cream with chocolate hazelnut spread until it just holds its shape, then spoon on to eclair bases and top with the iced tops.

★ The choux buns will keep for 2 days, unfilled, in a cake tin. Recrisp in the oven before filling.

RECIPE AND FOOD STYLING: MITZIE WILSON PROP STYLING: SUE ROWLANDS PHOTO: TOBY SCOTT

Cheesecake-swirled BROWNIES

These make a lovely change from traditional brownies – they are not as rich but are equally delicious!

MAKES 12-16 **PREP** 15 MINS **BAKE** 30 MINS

RECIPE, FOOD AND PROP STYLING: MITZIE WILSON PHOTO: TOBY SCOTT

FOR THE BROWNIES

- 100g butter, cut into cubes
- 100g plain chocolate, roughly chopped
- 125g caster sugar
- Pinch of salt
- 3 medium eggs, beaten
- 75g self-raising flour
- 1tbsp cocoa powder

FOR THE CHEESECAKE

- 200g plain chocolate, chopped (or use chocolate chips)
- 200g cream cheese
- 2 medium egg yolks
- 75g caster sugar

YOU WILL NEED

- A 26cm x 18cm tin, lined with baking parchment

★ Preheat oven to gas mark 4/180°C (160°C in a fan oven).

★ Place butter and chocolate in a medium saucepan and melt over a low heat. Stir constantly until smooth, then remove from the heat and beat in sugar and salt. Beat in eggs, 1 at a time, until smooth, then add flour and cocoa powder and beat until smooth. Add mixture to the tin.

★ **TO MAKE CHEESECAKE** In a clean bowl, beat together all the ingredients until smooth. Dollop on to brownie mixture, then swirl mixtures together lightly with a knife. Don't over mix, as it is nice to see and taste the 2 different mixtures.

★ Bake for 30 mins or until the middle of the cake is just set – it should still have a slight wobble to it but, if you prefer it less gooey, bake for a further 5 mins.

★ Allow to cool in the tin, then cut into squares to serve.

Chocolate + crushed violet
MADELEINES

*These French cakes are rich and buttery. Try them dipped
in melted chocolate – a chocoholic's dream*

MAKES 9-12 **PREP** 20 MINS **BAKE** 15 MINS

FOR THE CHOUX
- 50g butter, melted, plus extra for greasing
- 50g plain flour, plus extra for dusting
- 1 medium egg
- 50g caster sugar
- 1tbsp cocoa powder
- ¼tsp baking powder
- ½tsp vanilla extract

TO DECORATE
- 150g icing sugar
- Drop of violet extract (available from Lakeland)
- Purple food colouring
- Crystallised rose petal fragments (available from squires-shop.com)

YOU WILL NEED
- A 9-12 hole madeleine tray
- Baking parchment

★ Preheat oven to gas mark 4/180°C (160°C in a fan oven).

★ Grease madeleine tray with a little melted butter, coating every ridge. Dust with a little flour and tap out the excess.

★ Place egg and sugar in a bowl and whisk with an electric whisk until it is thick and has increased almost 3 times in volume.

★ Sift over remaining flour, plus the cocoa and baking powders and fold in. Gently fold in butter and vanilla extract until evenly combined, but don't over mix.

★ Divide mixture between moulds and bake for 12-15 mins or until just firm to the touch. Allow to cool for 5 mins, then remove from moulds and leave to cool on a wire rack.

★ **TO MAKE ICING,** mix icing sugar with just enough water to make a thick pouring consistency. Add violet extract and colouring, if you like.

★ Dip the end of each madeleine into the icing, sprinkle over a few crystallised petals and leave to set on baking parchment.

★ The madeleines can be stored for 2-3 days in a cake tin.

RECIPE, FOOD AND PROP STYLING: MITZIE WILSON **PHOTO:** CLARE WINFIELD

Try this

If you don't have a heart tin, use a 20cm-square cake tin instead.

Caramel brownie
HEART

A dark and delicious cake to share with loved ones, whether with post-dinner coffee or as an indulgent dessert

SERVES 8-10 **PREP** 20 MINS **BAKE** 35 MINS

FOR THE CAKE
- 150g butter
- 200g plain chocolate
- 175g light muscovado sugar
- 3 large eggs
- 75g plain flour
- 50g caramel-filled chocolates

TO DECORATE
- A little caramel (we used Carnation Caramel)
- 50g plain chocolate, melted

YOU WILL NEED
- A 23cm heart-shaped cake tin, greased and lined

★ Preheat oven to gas mark 3/170°C (150°C in a fan oven).

★ Place butter and chocolate in a bowl. Set bowl over a pan of gently simmering water, making sure it does not touch the water. Heat, stirring gently, until melted. Remove bowl from the pan and leave to cool slightly.

★ Beat sugar into chocolate mixture with a wooden spoon, then beat in eggs, one at a time, until mixture is smooth. Add flour, beat until evenly mixed, then add caramel-filled chocolates.

★ Pour mixture into tin and bake for 30-35 mins or until cake feels just firm to the touch in the centre.

★ Leave to cool, then turn out on to a plate and flip over. Drizzle over caramel and melted chocolate just before serving.

RECIPE, FOOD AND PROP STYLING: MITZIE WILSON PHOTO: CLARE WINFIELD

Black Forest
SLICE

This makes a stunning centrepiece – and everyone will want a slice!

SERVES 10   **PREP** 40 MINS   **BAKE** 15 MINS

FOR THE SPONGE
- 125g caster sugar
- 3 large eggs
- 100g plain flour
- 25g cocoa powder
- 2tbsp kirsch liqueur (optional)

FOR THE GANACHE
- 150ml whipping cream
- 200g plain chocolate
- 400g can cherries in natural juices
- 2tbsp seedless raspberry jam
- 200ml double cream

TO DECORATE
- A few fresh cherries
- A little plain chocolate, grated

YOU WILL NEED
- A 33cm x 23cm Swiss roll tin, greased and lined with baking parchment

★ Preheat oven to gas mark 6/200°C (180°C in a fan oven).

★ Put sugar and eggs into the bowl of an electric mixer and whisk for 10 mins until pale and thick enough to leave a trail when the whisk is lifted.

★ Sift flour and cocoa into mixture and fold in carefully using a large metal spoon.

★ Pour mixture into prepared tin and use a spatula to smooth evenly into corners. Bake in centre of oven for 10-12 mins until it has risen and is just firm to the touch. Leave to cool in tin. Sprinkle with kirsch, if you like.

★ **TO MAKE GANACHE,** heat whipping cream in a pan to a gentle simmer, then pour over chocolate and stir until smooth. Leave to cool and thicken.

★ Drain juice from can of cherries into a saucepan, then add jam and boil until reduced to 4tbsp. Add cherries and stir to coat.

★ Turn cake out of the tin, peel off the baking parchment, then trim off all edges. Cut in half down the middle to give 2 long slices of cake.

★ Spread half of the ganache over the top of 1 cake slice. Whip double cream until it just holds its shape, then spread two thirds of it over the ganache and top with drained cherries.

★ Place other cake slice on top and arrange remaining cream in dollops down the centre. Decorate with fresh cherries and grated chocolate or chocolate curls.

RECIPE AND FOOD STYLING: MITZIE WILSON   PROP STYLING: SUE ROWLANDS   PHOTO: TOBY SCOTT

Try this

You can make this cake alcohol-free by replacing the kirsch with 2tbsp orange juice.

Praline layer CAKE

This is a grown-up, boozy cake. The cake layers are soaked in hazelnut liqueur, then covered in a delicious cream and chocolate hazelnut icing

SERVES 12 **PREP** 50 MINS, PLUS SETTING **BAKE** 30 MINS

FOR THE SPONGE
- 225g plain chocolate, chopped
- 150g hazelnuts
- 300g butter, softened
- 300g caster sugar
- 7 medium eggs, beaten
- 150g self-raising flour
- 1½tsp baking powder

FOR THE SYRUP
- 35g caster sugar
- 2tbsp Frangelico or hazelnut liqueur

FOR THE FILLING
- 150ml double cream

TO DECORATE
- 300g chocolate hazelnut spread
- 300ml double cream
- 25g plain chocolate
- 9 chocolate hazelnut truffles

YOU WILL NEED
- 3 x 20cm cake tins, base lined with baking parchment

★ Preheat oven to gas mark 4/ 180°C (160°C in a fan oven).

★ Place 6tbsp water in a small pan and bring to the boil, then add chocolate and leave until melted. Stir until smooth and leave to cool while making the cake mixture.

★ Place hazelnuts in a food processor and blend until finely ground, but don't over mix or they may become oily.

★ Place butter and sugar in a mixing bowl and beat until light and creamy. Gradually beat in eggs, adding a little flour if the mixture begins to curdle.

★ Stir in hazelnuts and melted chocolate, then fold in the rest of the flour and the baking powder until mixed.

★ Divide mixture between tins and bake for 25-30 mins until they have risen and are firm to the touch. Allow to cool in tins for 10 mins, then run a knife around the inside of the tins to release cakes and turn out on to a wire rack to cool completely.

★ **TO MAKE SYRUP,** place sugar in a pan with 2tbsp water and bring to the boil, then simmer for 1 min until syrupy. Pour in liqueur.

★ **TO MAKE FILLING,** whisk double cream until thick, then use to sandwich the 3 cakes on top of each other, placing the last cake upside down to give a flat top.

★ **TO DECORATE,** whisk chocolate hazelnut spread and cream together until thick, then chill for at least 15 mins to allow it to thicken slightly. Spread over top and sides of cake, then put in the fridge to allow icing to set.

★ Melt chocolate in a bowl over gently simmering water, then drizzle over the top of the cake and add truffles.

★ The cake will keep for up to 1 week in the fridge.

RECIPE, FOOD AND PROP STYLING: MITZIE WILSON PHOTO: CLARE WINFIELD

Chocolate TARTLETS

These are much easier to make than they look, using ready-made shortcrust pastry and a very simple filling. Top with fresh fruit, if you prefer

MAKES 12 **PREP** 25 MINS, PLUS SETTING **BAKE** 15 MINS

FOR THE PASTRY
- 375g pack sweet dessert pastry

FOR THE FILLING
- 150ml double cream
- 1tbsp runny honey
- 100g plain chocolate (60% cocoa solids)
- 50g butter

FOR THE DECORATION
- 50g white chocolate
- A few milk chocolate drops

YOU WILL NEED
- 8cm round pastry cutter
- 12-hole shallow bun tray
- Baking parchment
- Baking beans
- A small plastic piping bag

★ Roll out pastry to the thickness of a £1 coin. Using a round pastry cutter, cut out 12 circles and use to line bun trays. Prick bases with a fork and chill for 10 mins. You will have some left over pastry, which you can use to make jam tarts or keep for another time (it will freeze for up to 3 months).

★ Preheat oven to gas mark 6/200°C (180°C in a fan oven). Line each pastry case with a circle of baking parchment and fill with baking beans. Bake for 12-14 mins until golden, then remove parchment and beans and leave to cool on a wire rack.

★ **TO MAKE FILLING,** place cream and honey in a pan and bring to the boil. Remove from the heat and add chocolate, stirring until melted. Add butter and stir until smooth. Allow to cool a little, then pour mixture into pastry cases and leave to set in the fridge (for about 1 hr).

★ **TO DECORATE,** make daisies by melting white chocolate in a small bowl over a pan of gently simmering water. Place in a piping bag and allow to cool until thick enough to pipe, then snip off the end of the bag. Lay a sheet of baking parchment on to a tray and pipe daisy shapes, adding a choc chip in the centre. Chill until set, then carefully place on top of the tartlets.

★ The tartlets will keep for up to 3 days in the fridge.

RECIPE, FOOD AND PROP STYLING: MITZIE WILSON PHOTO: TOBY SCOTT

Try this
Fill it with whipped cream and fresh fruit if you prefer, or with hazelnut cream (see page 117)

Chocolate meringue
ROULADE

Wonderfully light and creamy, this is a perfect end to any dinner party

SERVES 8 **PREP** 25 MINS, PLUS CHILLING **BAKE** 20 MINS

RECIPE, FOOD AND PROP STYLING: MITZIE WILSON PHOTO: TOBY SCOTT

FOR THE MERINGUE
- 4 medium egg whites
- 250g caster sugar
- 1tsp cornflour
- 1tsp white wine vinegar
- 2tsp cocoa powder
- Icing sugar, for dusting

FOR THE FILLING
- 150g white chocolate, very finely chopped
- 150g butter, at room temperature

FOR THE TOPPING
- 25g plain chocolate

YOU WILL NEED
- A 30cm x 20cm Swiss roll tin, lined with baking parchment

★ Preheat oven to gas mark 3/170°C (150°C in a fan oven).

★ Place egg whites in a clean grease-free bowl and whisk with an electric whisk until stiff, then gradually add caster sugar, whisking until thick and glossy. Whisk in cornflour, vinegar and cocoa powder. Add to tin, spread evenly with a spatula and bake for 20 mins until the top is golden. Don't worry if the meringue puffs up a bit.

★ **TO MAKE FILLING,** place white chocolate in a bowl over a pan of gently simmering water (make sure bowl does not touch the water) and leave to melt. Remove bowl from pan and leave chocolate to cool for 10 mins. Whisk butter until smooth and creamy, then gradually whisk in cooled chocolate. Chill for at least 1 hr or until it has thickened, then whisk again until it just holds its shape.

★ When roulade is cooked, dust a sheet of baking parchment with icing sugar. Leave meringue to cool for 5 mins, then turn out on to baking parchment and peel off backing parchment. Leave meringue to cool completely.

★ Spread filling over meringue and roll up from the short end, using the baking parchment to help.

★ **FOR THE TOPPING,** place on a serving plate, seam side down. Melt chocolate (as above) and drizzle over.

★ This will keep for up to 3-4 days in the fridge.

Chocolate brandy
PROFITEROLES

Truly indulgent, make these even more divine by flavouring the whipped ganache filling with your favourite liqueur – try Irish cream, rum or Frangelico

SERVES 6 PREP 15 MINS BAKE 25 MINS

FOR THE CHOUX
- 50g butter, diced
- 4tbsp milk
- 1tsp caster sugar
- 85g plain flour
- 15g cocoa powder
- 3 medium eggs, beaten

FOR THE FILLING
- 75g butter
- 100ml double cream
- 2tbsp light muscovado sugar
- 100g plain chocolate (70% cocoa solids), finely chopped
- 1tbsp brandy or liqueur

FOR THE CHOCOLATE SAUCE
- 4tbsp cocoa powder
- 4tbsp golden syrup
- 15g butter

TO DECORATE
- Edible gold lustre powder

YOU WILL NEED
- A large piping bag, fitted with a large plain nozzle
- 2 baking sheets, lightly greased

★ Preheat oven to gas mark 6/ 200°C (180°C in a fan oven).

★ Place butter, milk, caster sugar and 4tbsp cold water in a medium saucepan over a low heat until butter has melted, then bring to the boil.

★ Add all the flour and cocoa powder in one go and beat well with a wooden spoon until mixture forms a soft ball and comes away from the sides of the pan. Remove from the heat and leave to cool for 5 mins.

★ Gradually add eggs, a little at a time, beating into mixture. At first, it will look scrambled, but the more you beat it, the smoother it will become. The mixture will be smooth and shiny, hold its shape and be a thick dropping consistency when it's ready.

★ Place mixture in a large piping bag fitted with a large plain nozzle. Pipe small rounds (each about the size of a whole walnut) on baking sheets.

★ Bake for 15-20 mins until they have risen and are crisp. Remove from oven, then cut a slit in the side of each to allow steam to escape. Return buns to the hot oven for a further 4-5 mins to dry out. Remove and leave to cool, then cut almost in half.

★ **TO MAKE FILLING,** melt butter in a small pan, add cream and sugar and stir until sugar has dissolved. Add chocolate and leave for 5 mins until melted, then stir until smooth. Allow to cool until it has thickened, then add brandy and whisk until much paler in colour. Place in a piping bag and pipe between split profiteroles.

★ **TO MAKE SAUCE,** place all the ingredients in a small pan and heat until butter has melted and mixture is smooth. Serve it hot or cold, poured over the profiteroles, then dust them with gold lustre, if you like.

RECIPE, FOOD AND PROP STYLING: MITZIE WILSON PHOTO: TOBY SCOTT

Try this

For an added kick, replace the cardamom with ½tsp ground black pepper or a pinch of chilli flakes.

Cardamom chocolate
TORTE

Rich, dense and delicately spiced, this will be a hit at any dinner party

SERVES 12   PREP 20 MINS   BAKE 30 MINS

RECIPE, FOOD AND PROP STYLING: MITZIE WILSON PHOTO: TOBY SCOTT

FOR THE TORTE

- 20 green cardamom pods
- 225g plain chocolate
- 5 medium eggs, separated
- 175g caster sugar
- 150g ground almonds
- Crème fraîche, to serve

FOR THE SAUCE

- 125ml maple syrup
- 50g plain chocolate
- A knob of butter

YOU WILL NEED

- A 20cm round springform cake tin, base lined with baking parchment
- A pestle and mortar

★ Preheat oven to gas mark 3/170°C (150°C in a fan oven).

★ Lightly bash cardamom, using a pestle and mortar, to open pods, then discard skins and crush seeds a little.

★ Melt chocolate in a heatproof bowl set over a pan of simmering water, then allow to cool slightly.

★ Whisk egg whites in a clean bowl until they form soft peaks. Gradually whisk in half of the sugar, 1tbsp at time, until meringue is smooth and shiny.

★ Place egg yolks and remaining sugar in a bowl and whisk until it is pale and has doubled in volume. Add a generous spoonful of meringue and mix well, then fold in melted chocolate and rest of meringue mixture. Finally, fold in ground almonds and cardamom seeds, taking care not to knock out all the air in the mixture.

★ Spoon mixture into tin and bake for 30 mins. Turn off the oven and leave torte inside for 15 mins – it will continue cooking as it cools. Remove from oven and leave to cool in tin – the torte may sink a little and crack slightly, but that is part of its charm.

★ **TO MAKE SAUCE,** heat syrup in a small pan, then add chocolate and stir until melted. Beat in butter until smooth. Serve hot, poured over slices of torte, with crème fraîche on the side.

Chocolate, cherry + pistachio
FUDGE

A treat that's so easy to make and makes a great gift, too

MAKES 24 CUBES **PREP** 15 MINS, PLUS SETTING **BAKE** NONE

FOR THE FUDGE
- 25g butter
- 400g plain chocolate, broken into chunks
- 397g can sweetened condensed milk
- 100g icing sugar
- 50g pistachios
- 100g dried sour cherries
- 50g white chocolate chips

YOU WILL NEED
- 900g loaf tin, lined with foil

★ Place butter, chocolate and condensed milk into a pan and heat very gently until chocolate has melted.

★ Stir in icing sugar, pistachios and dried cherries, then cool for a few minutes before adding white chocolate chips.

★ Spoon mixture into the tin and leave in the fridge for a few hours until set. Turn out and cut into small squares.

RECIPE AND FOOD STYLING: MITZIE WILSON **PROP STYLING:** SUE ROWLANDS **PHOTO:** TOBY SCOTT

The joy of
SAVOURY

*Delicious ideas whether for al fresco dining in your garden
or on a picnic, or to enjoy as a light midweek meal*

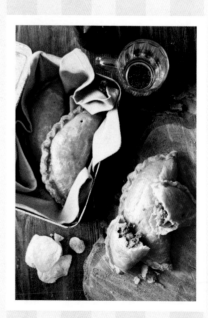

SHORTCRUST PASTRY

● **275g plain flour** ● **150g cold butter, cut into cubes**

★ Add flour to a large bowl, then using your fingertips, rub in butter until mixture resembles breadcrumbs. ★ Now add a splash of ice-cold water (best to add it very slowly, a little at a time) and start to gather the pastry together until it comes away from the edges of the bowl.
★ Turn out dough on to a lightly floured board, then pat into a flat round and cover with cling film. Put in the fridge to rest for 30 mins before you use it.

Crab + watercress SUMMER TART

Fresh crabmeat makes this easy-to-make tart a luxurious lunch or light dinner

SERVES 8 PREP 20 MINS BAKE 55 MINS

RECIPE, FOOD AND PROP STYLING: HEATHER WHINNEY PHOTO: WILLIAM SHAW

FOR THE TART CASE
- 500g pack shortcrust pastry (there may be some left over) or make your own (see left)

FOR THE FILLING
- 1tbsp olive oil
- 1 onion, finely chopped
- 50g Parmesan, grated
- 2 x 100g pots of fresh white crabmeat
- 70g bag watercress, roughly chopped
- Pinch of freshly grated nutmeg
- 4-5tbsp crème fraîche
- 2 eggs
- Pinch of paprika
- Tub of salad cress, snipped, to garnish (optional)

YOU WILL NEED
- A 20.5cm round, loose bottom flan tin
- Baking parchment
- Baking beans

★ Preheat oven to gas mark 6/200°C (180°C in a fan oven).

★ **TO MAKE TART CASE** Roll out pastry on a lightly floured board, then use to line tin – drape pastry over edge of tin, carefully pushing it into the sides, leaving a little overhang (you can trim this once cooked). Fill with baking parchment and baking beans and put in the oven for about 15 mins until edges are beginning to turn golden.

★ Remove from oven. Take out baking beans and parchment and return to oven for 1-2 mins to crisp up base. Remove and put to one side. Turn down the oven to gas mark 4/180°C (160°C in a fan oven).

★ **TO MAKE FILLING,** heat oil in a frying pan. Add onion and season well. Cook for 1-2 mins until soft, then put to one side to cool. Tip cooled onion into pastry base, spread out and sprinkle over half of the Parmesan. Add crabmeat and watercress and stir together a little, so evenly mixed. Sprinkle over nutmeg.

★ Mix together crème fraîche, eggs, paprika and remaining Parmesan and season, then pour mixture into tart case.

★ Bake for 30-35 mins until pastry is a pale golden colour and mixture is cooked. Remove from oven and leave to cool.

★ Garnish with cress, if using, and serve at room temperature with a salad, if you like.

Cheat's
PORK PIES

Try your hand at making these quintessential English pies – they will taste so much better than shop-bought ones

MAKES 6 **PREP** 30 MINS **BAKE** 1 HR 30 MINS

FOR THE PASTRY
- 453g plain flour, plus extra for dusting
- Pinch of salt
- 125g lard, cubed
- 125g butter, cubed

FOR THE FILLING
- 1tbsp olive oil
- 1 onion, finely chopped
- 400g pack pork tenderloin, finely chopped
- 4 slices of back bacon, finely chopped
- Pinch of freshly ground nutmeg
- 2-3 sage leaves, finely chopped

TO GLAZE
- 1 egg, beaten

YOU WILL NEED
- 14cm round cutter or small plate
- A 6-hole 5cm-deep nonstick muffin tin (9cm wide)
- A 10cm round cutter

★ Preheat oven to gas mark 7/220°C (200°C in a fan oven).

★ **TO MAKE PASTRY,** place flour and salt into a large bowl. Add lard and butter and rub in using your fingertips until it resembles fine crumbs. Trickle in enough cold water to bring mixture together to form a dough. Turn pastry out on to a lightly floured surface and knead into a ball. Flatten and chill in fridge while you prepare filling mixture.

★ **TO MAKE FILLING,** heat oil in a frying pan and add onion. Season well and cook for 2-3 mins until soft. Set aside and leave to cool. Tip tenderloin and bacon into a bowl, then add cooled onion, nutmeg, sage and plenty of freshly ground black pepper. Mix well.

★ Roll out pastry on a floured board (don't roll it too thin or it will be difficult to work with). Cut out 6 large circles, using a 14cm cutter or a small plate, and use to line muffin tin, allowing pastry to overlap the top of the tin a little. Divide pork mixture between pastry cases.

★ Re-roll any pastry and cut out 6 tops, using the 10cm cutter. Brush overhanging pastry with water. Sit pastry tops on pies and press to seal. Trim and pinch around edges to neaten. Brush with egg wash and bake for 20-30 mins until golden brown.

★ Reduce oven temperature to gas mark 4/180°C (160°C in a fan oven) and cook for 1 hr. If top is browning too much, cover loosely with foil.

★ Remove from tin and leave to cool a little, then run a knife around pies to loosen and remove from tin. Serve with piccalilli.

RECIPE, FOOD AND PROP STYLING: HEATHER WHINNEY PHOTO: WILLIAM SHAW

Try this

No time to make pastry?
Use a 500g pack of
ready-made shortcrust
pastry instead.

Ham, spinach + Stilton TART

The classic pairing of ham and cheese is made sophisticated by using Stilton

SERVES 8-10   **PREP** 30 MINS   **BAKE** 50 MINS

RECIPE, FOOD AND PROP STYLING: HEATHER WHINNEY **PHOTO**: WILLIAM SHAW

FOR THE TART CASE
- 500g pack shortcrust pastry
- Flour, for dusting

FOR THE FILLING
- 2tbsp olive oil
- 1 red onion, sliced
- 300g spinach leaves
- 75g good-quality ham, cut into chunks
- Handful of fresh basil leaves, torn (optional)
- 50g Stilton, crumbled
- 100ml milk
- 2 eggs
- Pinch of chilli flakes (optional)

YOU WILL NEED
- A 28cm x 18cm loose bottom tart tin
- Baking parchment
- Baking beans

★ Preheat oven to gas mark 6/200°C (180°C in a fan oven).

★ **TO MAKE TART CASE** Roll out pastry on a lightly floured surface and use to line tin, allowing it to overlap the edges, then secure and trim. Line with baking parchment and baking beans and bake for 15-20 mins until edges are a pale golden colour. Remove beans and parchment and put tart case to one side. Turn down oven to gas mark 4/180°C (160°C in a fan oven).

★ **FOR THE FILLING,** heat half of the olive oil in a large frying pan and add onion. Season with sea salt and freshly ground black pepper and cook for 3-4 mins until soft, then spoon over pastry base. Add spinach to pan on a very low heat and cook gently until it wilts — sprinkle over a few drops of water, if needed. Drain well, then arrange on top of onions. Top with ham, tucking it in-between spinach a little. Scatter over basil, if using, and Stilton.

★ Mix together milk and eggs and add most of the chilli flakes, if using. Season, then carefully pour over tart. Drizzle over remaining oil and bake in oven for 20-30 mins or until mixture has set. Remove and leave to cool. Sprinkle over remaining chilli flakes, if you like, then slice and serve.

Spinach, bacon + cheese SCONES

Packed with flavour, these scones are perfect with a simple salad or alongside soup for an easy yet delicious lunch

SERVES 8   PREP 15 MINS   BAKE 20 MINS

FOR THE SCONES

- 4 rashers streaky bacon, snipped into little pieces
- 225g self-raising flour, plus extra for dusting
- ½tsp salt
- Pinch of mustard powder
- 50g butter
- 50g baby spinach leaves, finely chopped
- 50g Cheddar, grated
- 150ml milk

YOU WILL NEED

- A baking tray

★ Preheat oven to gas mark 7/220°C (200°C in a fan oven).

★ Dry-fry bacon until crispy, then set aside to cool.

★ Place flour, salt and mustard in a bowl. Add butter and rub together with your fingertips until mixture resembles breadcrumbs. Stir in spinach, bacon and cheese (or place everything in a food processor and blend together). Pour in milk and mix together with a knife until it forms a soft dough.

★ Turn out dough on to a lightly floured worktop and knead lightly into a circle about 3cm thick. Place on baking tray and score into 8 triangles.

★ Bake for 15-20 mins until the scones are golden brown and sound hollow when tapped underneath. Serve warm or cold with chutney, if you like.

RECIPE, FOOD AND PROP STYLING: MITZIE WILSON PHOTO: TOBY SCOTT

Try this

For ease, you can use roasted peppers from a jar instead.

Pepper + goats' cheese TART

Bursting with wonderfully colourful and delicious vegetables

SERVES 8-12 **PREP** 30 MINS **BAKE** 50 MINS

RECIPE, FOOD AND PROP STYLING: HEATHER WHINNEY PHOTO: WILLIAM SHAW

FOR THE FILLING

- 4 red peppers
- 2tbsp olive oil
- 3 courgettes, trimmed, halved lengthways and chopped
- 2 cloves of garlic, finely chopped
- Few sprigs of rosemary, finely chopped
- Handful of cherry tomatoes, halved
- 75g medium soft goats' cheese, torn
- 100ml double cream
- 2 eggs

FOR THE PASTRY

- 500g pack shortcrust pastry
- A little flour, for dusting

YOU WILL NEED

- A 20.5cm round, loose bottom tart tin
- Baking parchment
- Baking beans

★ Preheat oven to gas mark 6/200°C (180°C in a fan oven).

★ Add peppers to a roasting tin, drizzle over half of the oil and roast for about 20 mins until just beginning to char. Remove and place in a plastic bag to cool.

★ Meanwhile, roll out pastry on a lightly floured board and use to line tin, allowing it to overlap the edge, then secure and trim. Fill with baking parchment and baking beans, then bake for 15-20 mins until just turning golden around the edges. Remove beans and parchment and set tart case to one side.

★ Reduce oven temperature to gas mark 4/180°C (160°C in a fan oven).

★ **TO MAKE FILLING,** heat remaining oil in a frying pan and add courgettes, garlic and rosemary. Cook for 6-8 mins until courgettes are beginning to soften and turn golden. Tip into the base of the tart.

★ Remove skins from peppers, roughly chop flesh and arrange in tart along with tomatoes and goats' cheese, ensuring that everything is evenly distributed.

★ In a jug, mix together cream and eggs. Season with sea salt and freshly ground black pepper and carefully pour over tart. Put in oven and cook for 20-30 mins or until mixture is set.

★ Remove and leave to cool before releasing from tin and slicing.

Cornish
PASTIES

These are proper pasties made with steak, potato, lots of pepper and swede in a firm yet crumbly pastry. They're worth the effort and freeze well, too

MAKES 9 PREP 30 MINS, PLUS RESTING BAKE 1 HR

FOR THE FILLING
- 400g chuck steak
- 2 large potatoes, peeled
- 1 small swede (about 250g), peeled
- 1 large onion, finely diced
- 1tsp salt
- 2-3tsp freshly ground black pepper

FOR THE PASTRY
- 500g strong white flour
- 125g butter, well chilled
- 125g lard, well chilled
- 1 egg, beaten

YOU WILL NEED
- A baking tray, greased

★ Preheat oven to gas mark 4/180°C (160°C in a fan oven).

★ **TO MAKE FILLING** Slice the steak thinly, then chop finely with a sharp knife.

★ Cut potato and swede into slices, then dice and add to meat, along with the onion. Season well with the salt and pepper.

★ **TO MAKE PASTRY,** place flour in a bowl and rub in the butter and lard until mixture looks like breadcrumbs (or blend together in a food processor). Pour in 180ml-210ml cold water, mixing with a knife until combined. Turn out on to a work surface and knead mixture slightly until smooth, then wrap in cling film and leave to rest for 30 minutes.

★ Divide pastry into 9 balls and roll out each into a circle (about 16cm in diameter). Spoon a little filling in the centre of a pastry circle. Brush a little water along the edge of half the pastry, then fold pastry over filling and press down well to seal. Crimp edge and place on baking tray. Repeat process with remaining pastry.

★ Brush pasties with egg, then bake for 50 mins-1 hr until the meat and vegetables are cooked. Eat hot or cold.

RECIPE, FOOD AND PROP STYLING: MITZIE WILSON PHOTO: TOBY SCOTT

Try this

These can be frozen for up to 3 months. Defrost overnight before reheating in a hot oven.

Raisin + caraway seed
BREAD

This is a quick and easy loaf to make and is so good with cheese

MAKES 1 **PREP** 20 MINS, PLUS PROVING **BAKE** 35 MINS

FOR THE BREAD

- 300g granary or country grain flour
- 200g rye flour
- 1tsp salt
- 1tbsp honey
- 2tsp caraway seeds
- 7g sachet easy bake yeast
- 2tbsp light olive oil
- 300ml hand-hot water
- 150g raisins

YOU WILL NEED

- A baking tray

★ Preheat oven to gas mark 7/220°C (200°C in a fan oven).

★ Mix together flours, salt, honey, caraway seeds and yeast in a large bowl. Add oil and water, then mix together until a soft dough starts to form.

★ Add raisins and knead dough until smooth and elastic – this can take up to 10 mins by hand or 5 mins in an electric mixer with a dough hook. Shape dough into an oval and place on a baking tray.

★ **TO PROVE,** cover dough loosely with oiled cling film and leave to rise in a warm place until doubled in size. Remove cling film and slash dough lengthways down the middle.

★ Bake bread for 15 mins, then reduce oven temperature to gas mark 6/200°C (180°C in a fan oven) and cook for a further 15-20 mins until the bread has risen, is golden brown and sounds hollow when tapped underneath.

RECIPE, FOOD AND PROP STYLING: MITZIE WILSON PHOTO: TOBY SCOTT

Asparagus + cheese TART

Make seasonal asparagus the star in this delicious tart

SERVES 6 **PREP** 30 MINS **BAKE** 55 MINS

FOR THE PASTRY

- 500g pack ready-made shortcrust pastry (or make your own, see p128)
- A little flour, for dusting

FOR THE TOPPING

- ½tbsp olive oil
- 1 onion, finely chopped
- 2 cloves of garlic, finely chopped
- 25g Parmesan cheese, finely grated (optional)
- 3 x 110g packs fine asparagus, stalks trimmed if tough and woody
- 300ml double cream
- 100ml milk
- 3 eggs
- 75g Caerphilly cheese, grated
- Pinch of freshly grated nutmeg

YOU WILL NEED

- A 20.5cm x 30.5cm loose bottom oblong tin
- Baking parchment
- Baking beans
- A baking sheet

★ Preheat oven to gas mark 6/200°C (180°C in a fan oven).

★ **TO MAKE PASTRY CASE** Roll out pastry on a lightly floured board until just larger than tin. Drape over a rolling pin, then use to line tin, leaving pastry hanging over sides. Prick bottom with a fork, then line with baking parchment and fill with baking beans. Bake in oven for about 15 mins, until edges turn pale golden. Remove from oven, take out beans and parchment, and return pastry case to oven for 5 mins more (to ensure a crisp base).

★ Remove from oven and put aside to cool, still in the tin. Neaten pastry edges by trimming with a sharp knife. Turn down oven to gas mark 4/180°C (160°C in a fan oven).

★ **TO MAKE TOPPING,** heat oil in a small frying pan, add onion and cook for 1-2 mins until softened, then stir in garlic and cook for a further couple of mins. Leave to cool, then spread over pastry base. Scatter over Parmesan, if using.

★ Add asparagus to a pan of boiling, salted water and cook for about 4 mins, or until tender but still with a bite. Drain well and rinse in plenty of cold water (this will help to keep their colour and stop them from cooking any further). Leave to cool, then arrange them neatly in pastry base.

★ In a jug, mix together cream, milk, eggs and cheese, then season. Sit tart tin on a baking sheet, then slowly pour mixture over asparagus (there may be a little left over). Sprinkle over nutmeg, then bake for 30-35 mins, or until golden but still a little wobbly (it will continue to cook and set as it cools). Leave to cool slightly, then slice and serve.

RECIPE, FOOD AND PROP STYLING: HEATHER WHINNEY PHOTO: WILLIAM SHAW

Try this

If you trim pastry before baking, it may shrink, so leave it overhanging the side of the tin, then bake and trim.

Pizza SWIRLS

These are perfect for packed lunches or served with soup – and they freeze well, too

MAKES 12   **PREP** 30 MINS, PLUS PROVING   **BAKE** 20 MINS

FOR THE DOUGH

- 500g strong white bread flour
- 7g sachet easy bake yeast
- 1tsp sugar
- 1tsp salt
- 1tbsp olive oil
- 300ml warm water

FOR THE FILLING

- 18 rashers streaky bacon, snipped
- 5-6tbsp tomato ketchup
- 1 roasted red pepper (from a jar), diced
- About 12 basil leaves
- 75g mozzarella
- 50g Parmesan, grated

YOU WILL NEED

- A baking tray

★ Preheat oven to gas mark 6/200°C (180°C in a fan oven).

★ **TO MAKE DOUGH,** place flour, yeast, sugar and salt in a mixing bowl. Add oil and water and mix to a smooth pliable dough. Turn out on to a work surface and knead for 10 mins until smooth and elastic (or mix for 5 mins in an electric mixer with a dough hook).

★ Meanwhile, dry-fry bacon until crispy.

★ Roll out dough to a rectangle (about 35cm x 25cm long). Spread over tomato ketchup and sprinkle over red pepper and bacon. Tear basil leaves and scatter over the top. Tear mozzarella into pieces and arrange on top, then sprinkle over Parmesan.

★ Roll up dough tightly from one long edge (like a Swiss roll), then slice into 12. Arrange on baking tray with a 2cm space between each slice to allow room for spreading. Cover with oiled cling film and leave in a warm place to rise for about 45 mins or until doubled in size.

★ Bake rolls for about 20 mins until they are golden brown and have risen. Serve hot or cold, or freeze for up to 1 month.

RECIPE, FOOD AND PROP STYLING: MITZIE WILSON **PHOTO:** TOBY SCOTT

Caramelised onion + garlic
PUFF TART

This uses so few ingredients, yet really packs in the flavour.
Serve with a salad as a dinner party starter

SERVES 8 **PREP** 50 MINS **BAKE** 40 MINS

FOR THE PASTRY
- 500g pack puff pastry
- A little flour, for dusting

FOR THE FILLING
- 1tbsp olive oil
- 500g bag shallots, peeled and left whole
- Small handful of thyme stalks, finely chopped
- 5 cloves of garlic, peeled
- 1tbsp balsamic vinegar
- 2tbsp crème fraîche
- 2 eggs

YOU WILL NEED
- A 20.5cm x 30.5cm loose bottom oblong tin
- Baking parchment
- Baking beans

★ Preheat oven to gas mark 6/200°C (180°C in a fan oven).

★ **TO MAKE TART CASE,** roll out pastry on a lightly floured board and use to line tin, allowing it to overlap the edge, then secure and trim. Line with baking parchment and baking beans and bake for 15-20 mins until edges are beginning to turn golden. Remove beans and parchment and put tart case to one side.

★ Turn down oven to gas mark 4/180°C (160°C in a fan oven).

★ **TO MAKE FILLING,** heat oil in a heavy-based frying pan, then add shallots and half of the thyme. Season with sea salt and freshly ground black pepper and cook for about 10 mins – moving them around pan occasionally so they don't burn – until they start to colour.

★ Add garlic and balsamic and cook for a further 5 mins, then add 1-2tbsp water and cook for 10 mins more until onions are soft and caramelised and balsamic and water have evaporated.

★ Arrange shallots and garlic in tart base, then sprinkle over remaining thyme. Mix together crème fraîche and eggs, then pour over shallots, making sure it goes into all the gaps.

★ Bake for about 20 mins or until set and golden. Remove from the oven and leave to rest for at least 10 mins before releasing it from the tin, if serving warm – or leave to cool completely.

RECIPE, FOOD AND PROP STYLING: HEATHER WHINNEY PHOTO: WILLIAM SHAW

Try this

You can bake the base and cook the onions in advance – just assemble when ready to serve.

Pepper puff PIE

*A rustic tart that takes hardly any time to make
– perfect for a midweek supper*

SERVES 6 PREP 25 MINS BAKE 30 MINS

FOR THE TOPPING
- 4 red peppers, deseeded and cut into wedges
- 2 yellow peppers, deseeded and cut into wedges
- 2tbsp olive oil
- 2 eggs
- 2tbsp crème fraîche
- 75g Gruyère cheese, grated
- 2 cloves of garlic, crushed
- 3tbsp chopped parsley

FOR THE PASTRY
- 375g pack ready-rolled puff pastry

YOU WILL NEED
- A baking sheet, greased

★ Preheat oven to gas mark 6/200°C (180°C in a fan oven).

★ Put peppers on a baking sheet, drizzle with olive oil and roast for 10 mins to soften. Tip peppers on to a sheet of greaseproof paper.

★ Unwrap pastry and put on baking sheet used to roast peppers. Scatter peppers over the centre of the pastry and gather pastry sides up and over to create a thick pastry rim.

★ Crack eggs into a jug, add crème fraîche and whisk together lightly with a fork. Add Gruyère, garlic and parsley and season generously with salt and freshly ground black pepper.

★ Carefully pour egg filling into the centre of the pie (over the peppers). Bake for 30 mins until pastry is crisp and golden.

RECIPE, FOOD AND PROP STYLING: FELICITY BARNUM-BOBB PHOTO: DAVID MUNNS

Red pepper + prosciutto STROMBOLI

This is an impressive loaf to take on a picnic or when you need to prepare lunch in advance

SERVES 12 **PREP** 20 MINS, PLUS PROVING **BAKE** 30 MINS

FOR THE DOUGH

- 425g strong white bread flour
- 7g sachet fast action or easy bake yeast
- 1tsp salt
- 1tsp sugar
- 1tbsp olive oil
- 300ml hand-hot water

FOR THE FILLING

- 4 slices prosciutto crudo (cooked Italian ham)
- 100g Gruyère cheese, grated
- 2 roasted red peppers (from a jar)
- A handful of baby spinach leaves

YOU WILL NEED

- A large non-stick baking tray, lightly greased

★ Place flour, yeast, salt and sugar in a large mixing bowl and add oil and water. Mix to a soft dough, then turn out on to a work surface and knead until smooth and elastic (this will take 10 mins by hand or 5 mins in an electric mixer with a dough hook).

★ Place dough on to baking tray and pat out to a rectangle about 30cm x 24cm. Arrange prosciutto over dough and sprinkle over most of the cheese. Drain red peppers, pat dry and cut them open like a book, then lay them on top of the cheese. Scatter over spinach leaves.

★ Roll up dough from one long end, like a Swiss roll, tucking in spinach leaves, and making sure that the seam is underneath. Cover with oiled cling film and leave to prove until doubled in size.

★ Heat oven to gas mark 7/220°C (200°C in a fan oven).

★ Sprinkle remaining cheese over the top of the stromboli and bake for 30 mins until dough has risen and is golden brown. Leave to cool for 10 mins, then place on a wire rack and leave to cool completely. Serve it sliced.

RECIPE, FOOD AND PROP STYLING: MITZIE WILSON **PHOTO:** DAN JONES

Sunblush tomato
FOCACCIA

Serve with an Italian supper or split and fill with Parma ham and rocket for delicious sandwiches

SERVES 8 **PREP** 15 MINS, PLUS RISING **BAKE** 15 MINS

FOR THE FOCACCIA

- **500g strong white bread flour**
- **7g sachet fast action or easy bake yeast**
- **1tsp sugar**
- **1tsp salt**
- **100g sunblush tomatoes in olive oil**
- **300ml hand-hot water**
- **2-3 sprigs of rosemary, leaves picked**
- **1tsp sea salt flakes**

YOU WILL NEED

- **A baking tray**

★ Preheat oven to gas mark 7/220°C (200°C in a fan oven).

★ Place flour, yeast, sugar and salt in a large mixing bowl. Add 2tbsp oil from sunblush tomatoes and the water. Mix to a soft dough, then knead for 10 mins by hand, or for 5 mins in an electric mixer with a dough hook, until dough is smooth and elastic.

★ Drizzle a baking tray with 1tbsp oil from sunblush tomatoes, then turn out dough on to baking tray and pat out to a rectangle about 1cm thick. Cover with oiled cling film and leave in a warm place until doubled in size – this may take 40-60 mins depending on the warmth of the room.

★ When dough has risen, poke dimples in it with your fingertips, then arrange sunblush tomatoes and rosemary in the holes. Drizzle with another 2tbsp olive oil from the tomatoes and bake for 12-15 mins until it is golden and has risen. Cover top with foil halfway through cooking if tomatoes are browning too much. Sprinkle with sea salt and cut into squares to serve.

RECIPE, FOOD AND PROP STYLING: MITZIE WILSON PHOTO: DAN JONES

Smoked fish + baby leek
FLAN

Sweet leeks and spring onions complement the smokiness of the fish

SERVES 6-8 **PREP** 30 MINS **BAKE** 50 MINS

FOR THE PASTRY
- 500g pack shortcrust pastry
- A little flour, for dusting

FOR THE FILLING
- 1-2tbsp olive oil
- 100g pack of baby leeks, trimmed and halved
- 1 bunch of spring onions, trimmed, sliced lengthways and roughly chopped
- Handful of fresh dill, chopped
- 300g smoked (undyed) haddock, skinned
- 100ml milk
- 100ml double cream
- 1tbsp crème fraîche
- 2 eggs

YOU WILL NEED
- A 20.5cm round, fluted, ceramic tart dish
- Baking parchment
- Baking beans

★ Preheat oven to gas mark 6/200°C (180°C in a fan oven).

★ **TO MAKE FLAN CASE,** roll out pastry on a lightly floured board. Use to line tart base, allowing it to overlap the edge, then secure and trim. Line with baking parchment and baking beans, then put in oven for 15-20 mins until just turning golden around edges. Remove beans and parchment and set aside.

★ Reduce oven temperature to gas mark 4/180°C (160°C in a fan oven).

★ **TO MAKE FILLING,** heat oil in a large frying pan and add leeks and spring onions. Season with sea salt and freshly ground black pepper and cook for 8-10 mins till soft and golden. Remove and put to one side, then stir though half of the dill.

★ Wipe out pan, then add haddock and milk – top up with a little water to just cover, if needed. Simmer gently for 5-8 mins until fish is opaque and cooked, then remove with a slotted spoon and break up into chunky pieces. Arrange haddock and leek mixture in base of flan.

★ Mix together cream, crème fraîche and eggs, then season. Pour over tart, sprinkle over remaining dill and put in oven for 20-30 mins or until just cooked and lightly golden – it will continue to set after you have removed it from the oven.

★ Leave for at least 10 mins before serving.

RECIPE, FOOD AND PROP STYLING: HEATHER WHINNEY **PHOTO**: WILLIAM SHAW

Olive + cheese
BREADSTICKS

Great to serve with drinks, or you could make them smaller to fit in a lunch box – either way, they will be devoured in minutes!

MAKES 8   PREP 20 MINS, PLUS PROVING   BAKE 20 MINS

FOR THE STICKS

- 500g strong white bread flour
- 2tsp salt
- 2tsp sugar
- 7g sachet easy bake yeast
- 3tbsp olive oil
- 50g Cheddar, grated
- 200g pitted olives, drained and patted dry
- A little sea salt
- 2tsp finely chopped rosemary

YOU WILL NEED

- 2 baking trays, oiled

★ Preheat oven to gas mark 7/220°C (200°C in a fan oven).

★ Place flour, salt and sugar into a mixing bowl and stir in yeast. Mix oil with 300ml hand-hot water and add to the flour. Mix together until it forms a soft dough, then turn out on to a work surface and knead for 10 mins (or 5 mins in an electric mixer with a dough hook).

★ Divide dough into 8 equal pieces and roll each into a sausage shape about 30cm in length. Roll each one in a little grated cheese and some olives, poking them into the bread.

★ Place breadsticks on baking trays. Cover with oiled cling film and leave in a warm place to prove for about 45 mins until they have risen a little.

★ Sprinkle with a little sea salt and chopped rosemary. Poke olives into the dough again, if necessary, so that they don't fall off when baked.

★ Bake breadsticks for 15 mins until golden brown, then cover with foil and bake for a further 5 mins. Leave to cool completely.

RECIPE, FOOD AND PROP STYLING: MITZIE WILSON PHOTO: TOBY SCOTT

Courgette + pine nut TART

A delicious meat-free alternative that looks and tastes fantastic

SERVES 8   **PREP** 20 MINS   **BAKE** 55 MINS

FOR THE PASTRY
- 500g pack shortcrust pastry (or make your own, if you like, see p128)
- A little flour, for dusting

FOR THE FILLING
- 2-3tbsp olive oil
- 2 red onions, finely sliced
- 3 cloves of garlic, finely sliced
- 3-4 courgettes, finely sliced
- About 50g Parmesan, grated
- Handful of pine nuts, lightly toasted
- A few thyme sprigs, leaves picked (optional)
- About 300ml double cream (top up with milk, if more is needed)
- 3 eggs

YOU WILL NEED
- A 20.5cm round, loose bottom deep flan tin
- Baking parchment
- Baking beans

★ Preheat oven to gas mark 6/200°C (180°C in a fan oven).

★ **TO MAKE PASTRY CASE,** roll out pastry on a lightly floured worktop into a large round (larger than the tin) and carefully lift into the tin, using a rolling pin. Tuck in and around the tin, allowing pastry to drape over the edge. Fill with baking parchment and baking beans and put in the oven for about 15 mins or until edges start to turn golden.

★ Remove from oven, take out beans and parchment and put back in the oven for a few mins to crisp the bottom. Remove and trim pastry edges. Put to one side. Turn down oven to gas mark 4/180°C (160°C in fan oven).

★ **TO MAKE FILLING,** heat half of the oil in a large frying pan, add onions, then season and cook for 1-2 mins. Stir in half of the garlic, cook for a few mins more until softened, then remove from the heat and set aside. Heat remaining oil in a pan, add courgettes and the remaining garlic and fry for 3 to 4 mins until softened. Remove from the heat and leave to cool.

★ Sprinkle Parmesan over pastry base and fill with onion mixture. Arrange courgettes in a neat pattern on top of onions and sprinkle over half of the pine nuts and thyme, if using.

★ Mix together cream and eggs, season and pour over tart, then top with the rest of the pine nuts. Put in the oven and cook for 35 to 40 mins until just set and golden. Remove and leave to cool a little before removing from tin to serve.

RECIPE, FOOD AND PROP STYLING: HEATHER WHINNEY PHOTO: WILLIAM SHAW

Try this

Make up to 2 days ahead and refrigerate. Warm in oven or serve at room temperature.

Try this

Top pretzels with bacon rashers or salami, sliced tomatoes and slices of cheese for the last few mins of cooking.

Home-made cheese
PRETZELS

These are briefly cooked in boiling water with bicarbonate of soda to give them a lovely dark brown colour

MAKES 12   PREP 30 MINS, PLUS PROVING   BAKE 20 MINS

RECIPE, FOOD AND PROP STYLING: MITZIE WILSON   PHOTO: TOBY SCOTT

FOR THE DOUGH
- 650g strong white bread flour
- 7g sachet easy bake yeast
- 1½tsp salt
- 1tbsp sugar

FOR THE GLAZE + TOPPING
- 2tbsp bicarbonate of soda
- 100g Cheddar, grated

YOU WILL NEED
- 2 baking trays, lined with baking parchment

★ Preheat oven to gas mark 7/220°C (200°C in a fan oven).

★ **TO MAKE DOUGH,** place flour, yeast, salt and sugar in a large mixing bowl. Add 400ml hand-hot water. Mix well to form a soft dough. Turn out and knead by hand for 10 mins (or for 5 mins in an electric mixer with a dough hook).

★ Divide dough into 12 equal pieces, then roll each piece into a long thin sausage about 45.5cm long. Fold the ends of 1 piece of dough over to make a loop halfway down the length. Twist the ends once, then fold the ends back so that they lie on the rounded part of the loop. Place on a baking tray and repeat process with remaining dough. Cover with oiled cling film and leave in a warm place for about 45 mins until doubled in size.

★ **TO MAKE GLAZE,** bring a large shallow pan of water to the boil, then stir in bicarbonate of soda. Add pretzels, one at a time, and cook for just 1 min, then turn over and cook for 1 min further to seal them. Remove with a slotted spoon and place on a baking tray. Bake for 12 mins until golden brown.

★ Remove pretzels from oven, sprinkle over cheese and return to the oven for a further 5 mins. These are best eaten the day they are made or warmed a little on the following day.

Butternut squash + sage
TART

This is equally delicious whether served warm or cold

SERVES 4-6 **PREP** 35 MINS, PLUS CHILLING **BAKE** 45 MINS

FOR THE PASTRY CASE
- 150g plain flour, plus extra for dusting
- 75g butter

FOR THE FILLING
- 300g butternut squash
- 25g baby spinach leaves, rinsed
- 75g goats' cheese
- 3 sage leaves, chopped
- 200ml double cream
- 2 eggs

YOU WILL NEED
- A 20cm fluted flan tin
- Baking parchment
- Baking beans

★ Preheat oven to gas mark 6/200°C (180°C in a fan oven).

★ **TO MAKE PASTRY CASE,** place flour and butter in a food processor and blend until mixture looks like breadcrumbs. Add 3tbsp water and blend again (adding a little extra cold water, if needed). Turn out mixture on to a work surface, and knead slightly, bringing it into a ball. Chill for 15 mins.

★ Peel and dice butternut squash, then roast in the oven for about 15 mins or until just tender.

★ Dust a work surface with flour, then roll out pastry thinly until large enough to line flan tin. Lift pastry into the tin, trim the edges and line with baking parchment and baking beans. Bake for 15 mins, then remove parchment and beans.

★ Add butternut squash and spinach to pastry case. Crumble goats' cheese over the top and scatter over sage.

★ Beat together cream and eggs with plenty of seasoning and pour into the tin. Bake for 25-30 mins or until the mixture is golden and the custard is just set.

RECIPE, FOOD AND PROP STYLING: MITZIE WILSON **PHOTO:** TOBY SCOTT

Try this

If you prefer a plain loaf, simply omit the dates and walnuts.

Date + walnut wheaten
BREAD

This is a quick and easy bread to make, as it is made without yeast. It is delicious served with cheese

SERVES 8-10 **PREP** 15 MINS **BAKE** 45 MINS

FOR THE BREAD

- 225g wholemeal flour
- 75g plain flour
- 1½tsp bicarbonate of soda
- ½tsp salt
- 75g dried dates, chopped
- 50g walnuts, chopped
- 225ml natural yoghurt
- 2tbsp lemon juice
- 1tbsp honey
- 175ml milk

YOU WILL NEED

- A 900g loaf tin, greased and lined with baking parchment

★ Preheat oven to gas mark 8/230°C (210°C in a fan oven).

★ Place flours, bicarbonate of soda and salt into a mixing bowl with the dates and walnuts.

★ Mix together yoghurt, lemon juice, honey and milk, then stir into flour to make a soft dough. Place mixture in baking tin and smooth the top lightly.

★ Bake for 10 mins, then reduce oven temperature to gas mark 6/200°C (180°C in a fan oven) and bake for a further 25-35 mins until it is golden and firm to the touch and a skewer comes out clean when inserted into the centre. Turn out bread on to a wire rack to cool – it should sound hollow when the base is tapped. Slice and serve buttered.

★ This bread will keep for 2 days in a plastic bag.

RECIPE, FOOD AND PROP STYLING: MITZIE WILSON **PHOTO**: DAN JONES

Polenta + chorizo BUNS

These make a moreish savoury addition to an afternoon tea

MAKES 12 **PREP** 15 MINS **BAKE** 20 MINS

FOR THE BUNS
- 100g self-raising flour
- 75g quick cooking polenta meal
- 1tsp baking powder
- ½tsp salt
- 50g chorizo sausage, diced
- 25g sunblush tomatoes, drained and chopped
- 50g Cheddar, finely diced
- 25g Parmesan, grated
- 50g butter, melted
- 150ml milk
- 1 egg, beaten

YOU WILL NEED
- A shallow bun tin, lightly greased

★ Preheat oven to gas mark 6/200°C (180°C in a fan oven).

★ Place all the ingredients in a large mixing bowl and stir until a soft consistency (it will be quite wet initially). Leave to stand for 5 mins so that the polenta swells and the mixture develops a soft dropping consistency.

★ Drop tablespoonfuls into bun tin and bake for 15-20 mins or until they have risen and are golden brown.

★ The buns will keep for 1-2 days wrapped in foil.

RECIPE, FOOD AND PROP STYLING: MITZIE WILSON **PHOTO:** DAN JONES

The joy of
SPECIAL
OCCASIONS

Celebrate everything from birthdays to a new home with these stunning bakes

Allotment carrot CAKE

This cute carrot-topped version of an old favourite is great for a big gathering —and gardening enthusiasts will love it!

SERVES 16 **PREP** 20 MINS, PLUS 24 HRS DRYING **BAKE** 45 MINS

FOR THE CAKE

- 150g raisins
- Juice and zest of 1 orange
- 300g plain wholewheat flour
- 2tsp baking powder
- 1tsp mixed spice
- 1tsp ground cinnamon
- 175g golden caster sugar
- 175g coarsely grated carrots
- 75g pecans, finely chopped
- 3 large eggs
- 120ml sunflower oil
- 100ml milk

FOR THE ICING

- 100g softened butter
- 150g cream cheese
- 50g icing sugar

FOR THE CARROTS

- Sugar paste
- Green and orange paste food colourings

YOU WILL NEED

- A 20cm square cake tin, lined with baking parchment

★ Preheat oven to gas mark 4/180°C (160°C in a fan oven).

★ Soak the raisins in orange juice and zest.

★ **TO MAKE THE CAKE,** add flour, baking powder, spices and sugar to a large mixing bowl, then stir in carrots and pecans. Beat together eggs, oil and milk and add to the flour mixture, along with the raisin mixture. Stir well and pour into cake tin.

★ Bake for 35 to 45 mins until golden and just firm to the touch. Leave to cool in the tin for 10 mins, then turn out on to a wire rack and leave to cool completely.

★ **FOR THE ICING,** beat together butter and cream cheese until smooth, then beat in icing sugar. Cut the cake in half horizontally, spread half the icing over one half, then top with the second cake half. Spread the remaining icing over the top of the cake.

★ **TO MAKE CARROTS,** colour a little sugar paste with green food colouring and make pointed leaves. Colour the remaining sugar paste with orange food colouring and roll into tiny carrots, marking them with the back of a knife. Make a hole in the top of each one and add a sugar paste leaf. Leave to dry for 24 hours, then use to decorate the cake.

Almond cake flower GARLAND

This pretty floral cake is surprisingly easy to make. If you don't have flower cutters, just buy sugar flowers from the supermarket

SERVES 16   PREP 1 HR 20 MINS, PLUS OVERNIGHT DRYING   BAKE 40 MINS

FOR THE SPONGE
- 200g butter, softened, plus extra for greasing
- 200g golden caster sugar
- 4 eggs, beaten
- 100g self-raising flour
- 100g ground almonds
- 1tsp baking powder
- ½tsp almond extract

FOR THE FLOWERS
- Icing sugar, for dusting
- 75g each bright pink, yellow, orange and green ready-to-roll icing
- 200g royal icing sugar

YOU WILL NEED
- A 20cm-diameter ring mould, buttered and floured
- Blossom, daisy and leaf cutters in various sizes
- A piping bag with thick writing nozzle (or snip off the end of a plastic piping bag)

★ Preheat oven to gas mark 4/180°C (160°C in a fan oven).

★ **TO MAKE THE SPONGE,** place butter and sugar in a large mixing bowl and beat until smooth and creamy. Gradually beat in eggs, a little at a time, until smooth, adding a little flour if the mixture curdles. Add the remaining flour and the ground almonds, baking powder and almond extract and beat well until smooth. Spoon mixture into ring mould, spreading it out so it is level.

★ Bake for 30-40 minutes until it has risen and is firm and golden brown. A skewer should come out clean when inserted in the centre. Leave to cool for 10 mins in the tin, then turn out the cake and allow to cool on a wire rack.

★ **TO MAKE THE FLOWERS,** dust a work surface with icing sugar, then roll out the icing very thinly, one colour at a time. Cut out flowers and leaves using the cutters and leave to dry on crumpled kitchen paper overnight – or ideally for a couple of days. They will keep in an airtight container for weeks.

★ Make up the royal icing as directed on the pack and place in a piping bag. Pipe lines randomly over the cake, then attach the flowers and leaves.

★ The cake will keep for up to 1 week in a cake tin, but the flowers will become soft, so decorate it just before serving.

RECIPE, FOOD AND PROP STYLING: MITZIE WILSON **PHOTO:** CLARE WINFIELD

Lemon + rosemary LOAF

*The herb is an unusual but delicious addition to this cake
– serve when you invite friends round for tea*

SERVES 10 **PREP** 20 MINS **BAKE** 1 HR

FOR THE SPONGE

- 175g butter, at room temperature
- 175g caster sugar
- 3 medium eggs
- 200g self-raising flour
- 50g ground almonds
- Zest and juice of 1 lemon
- 1tsp finely chopped rosemary

FOR THE TOPPING

- 150g fondant icing sugar
- Few rosemary sprigs with flowers, to decorate
- Few coloured sugar-coated eggs (optional), to decorate

YOU WILL NEED

- A 900g loaf tin, greased and base lined with baking parchment

★ Preheat oven to gas mark 3/170°C (150°C in a fan oven).

★ Place butter and sugar in a large mixing bowl and beat with a wooden spoon or electric whisk until butter becomes a pale colour and mixture is light and fluffy.

★ Gradually beat in eggs, then fold in flour, ground almonds, lemon zest and juice and rosemary until evenly mixed.

★ Spoon mixture into loaf tin and bake for 1 hr until it has risen, is firm to the touch and is a pale golden colour. Leave to cool in the tin for 10 mins, then turn out on a wire rack and allow to cool completely.

★ **TO DECORATE,** mix icing sugar with 1-2 drops of cold water to make a very thick pouring consistency. Drizzle over cake and decorate with rosemary flowers and eggs, if you like.

RECIPE, FOOD AND PROP STYLING: MITZIE WILSON **PHOTO:** TOBY SCOTT

SERVES 16 **PREP** 1 HR **BAKE** 45 MINS

FOR THE SPONGE
- 400g butter, softened
- 400g caster sugar
- 1tsp vanilla extract
- 8 medium eggs, beaten
- 400g self-raising flour
- 1tsp baking powder

FOR THE BUTTERCREAM
- 3 large egg whites
- 250g caster sugar
- Pinch of salt
- Few drops of vanilla extract
- 300g unsalted butter, softened and cubed
- Green, yellow and pink food colourings

YOU WILL NEED
- 2 x 20cm round, deep cake tins, greased and lined with baking parchment
- A medium petal icing nozzle
- Piping bags
- A paintbrush

★ Preheat oven to gas mark 4/180°C (160°C in a fan oven).

★ **TO MAKE THE SPONGE,** place butter, sugar and vanilla in a bowl and beat with a wooden spoon or electric whisk until butter has become a pale colour and mixture is light and fluffy.

★ Add eggs, a little at a time, beating well after each addition. Sift together flour and baking powder – add 1-2tbsp of it to egg mixture, if mixture curdles. Fold in remaining flour with a large metal spoon. Divide mixture between the cake tins.

★ Bake for 35-45 mins. The mixture should be firm and a skewer should come out clean when inserted in the centre. If it doesn't, bake for a little longer. Allow to cool in the tin for 10 mins, then turn out and leave to cool completely.

★ **TO MAKE BUTTERCREAM,** add egg whites, sugar and salt to a bowl. Place bowl over a pan of gently simmering water, making sure that the bowl does not touch the water, and stir until sugar dissolves completely. Remove from the heat and pour into the bowl of an electric mixer. Whisk until thick and shiny, like a stiff meringue. Add vanilla and butter, a piece at a time, whisking continuously. The mixture will become runny, but keep whisking at full speed until it forms a fluffy buttercream.

★ If necessary, trim the tops of the cakes so they are level, then sandwich them together with about 4tbsp buttercream. Place on a plate and cover the top and sides thinly with buttercream. Chill for 10 mins, then cover with another layer of buttercream.

★ Colour 3tbsp buttercream with a little green food colouring and 1tbsp with yellow colouring, then cover and set aside. Colour the remaining buttercream pale pink. Fit petal nozzle in a piping bag, aligning the narrow end of the nozzle with the seam of the bag. Using a paintbrush, paint a stripe of pink colouring along the inside seam of the bag before carefully adding pale pink icing. Practise piping petals on a worktop first, with the stripe of darker colouring on the outside edge of petals.

★ Mark where each flower will sit, then pipe 1 heart-shaped petal. Repeat until you have 5 petals overlapping in a flower shape. Make 6 flowers. Place yellow icing in a small piping bag, snip off the end and pipe into the centre of each flower.

★ **TO MAKE LEAVES,** place green icing in a piping bag, snip off the end to make an upside down V-shape, then pipe leaves in-between flowers, applying pressure, then pulling the bag away to make a long leaf.

★ This cake can be kept chilled for 2-3 days in the fridge.

RECIPE, FOOD AND PROP STYLING: MITZIE WILSON **PHOTO:** CLARE WINFIELD

Buttercream rose
CAKE

Piped flowers make this a really pretty, eye-catching cake – perfect for spoiling a friend or celebrating Mother's Day

Flower pot CAKES

We filled ice cream cones with a white chocolate cake mixture, then topped them a white chocolate icing and sugar paste flowers

MAKES 12   **PREP** 1 HR, PLUS DRYING   **BAKE** 25 MINS

FOR THE CAKE
- 12 ice cream cone pots
- 150g butter
- 150g caster sugar
- 3 medium eggs, beaten
- ½tsp vanilla extract
- 125g self-raising flour
- 25g cocoa powder

FOR THE ICING
- 50g butter
- 75g white chocolate, melted
- 350g icing sugar, sifted, plus extra for dusting
- ½tsp vanilla extract
- A little green food colouring

FOR THE FLOWERS
- 250g lilac coloured sugar paste
- Edible pink dusting powder
- Rice paper butterflies (from cake shops)

YOU WILL NEED
- A cupcake tray
- A large piping bag and star nozzle
- 1 hydrangea cutter and veiner set (from design-a-cake.co.uk)
- A silicone mat

★ Preheat oven to gas mark 4/180°C (160°C in a fan oven).

★ Scrunch a strip of foil around the base of each ice cream cone, then place in cupcake tray, so they are packed in tightly.

★ In a mixing bowl, beat together butter and sugar until light and fluffy. Gradually add eggs and vanilla, then stir in flour and cocoa until evenly blended. Divide mixture between the ice cream cones (they should be a little more than half full).

★ Bake cakes for about 20-25 mins or until they have risen and are golden brown. Allow to cool in the tin.

★ **TO MAKE ICING,** beat butter until soft, then beat in chocolate, icing sugar and vanilla until smooth. Mix in green food colouring to the desired shade, then place in a piping bag with the star nozzle and pipe on top of cold cakes.

★ **TO MAKE FLOWERS,** dust work surface lightly with icing sugar and roll out the sugar paste thinly. Cut out 1 hydrangea at a time with a cutter, then place on a silicone mat and press petals together slightly to shape them. Leave to dry for a few hours (they can be made a couple of days in advance). Apply a little pink dusting powder to the centre of each flower and arrange a few on top of each cake with a rice paper butterfly.

RECIPE, FOOD AND PROP STYLING: MITZIE WILSON PHOTO: TOBY SCOTT

SERVES 20 **PREP** 2 HR 30 MINS **BAKE** 1 HR 10 MINS

FOR THE SPONGE

- 300g butter, at room temperature
- 400g caster sugar
- 2tsp vanilla extract
- 6 medium eggs, beaten
- 450g plain flour
- 3tsp baking powder
- 6tbsp hot water

FOR THE ICING

- 400g butter, softened
- 450g icing sugar, sifted, plus extra for dusting
- 2tsp vanilla extract
- Red, green, blue and yellow paste food colourings
- 150g white sugar paste
- 50g desiccated coconut (for the grass)

YOU WILL NEED

- A 20cm square deep cake tin, greased and lined with baking parchment.
- Piping bags and a set of nozzles
- A square cake board

★ Preheat oven to gas mark 4/180°C (160°C in a fan oven).

★ **TO MAKE THE SPONGE** Place butter, sugar and vanilla in a large bowl and beat with an electric mixer until light and fluffy. Beat in eggs, a little at a time, until mixture is smooth and light.

★ Beat in half of the flour and the baking powder, then carefully beat in the remaining flour and the hot water until well mixed.

★ Place mixture in cake tin and bake for 1 hr 10 mins. Check 10-15 mins before the end of baking time – the mixture should be firm in the centre and a skewer should come out clean when inserted in the centre. Allow to cool for 10 mins, then turn out of the tin and leave to cool completely.

★ Cut cake in half, down the middle, so you have 2 rectangular blocks. Trim 1 half so it's flat, and stack the rounded half on top of this. Cut a cube from the cake trimmings to make a chimney.

★ **TO MAKE ICING,** beat together butter, sugar and vanilla with a 2tsp hot water until light and creamy. Colour 200g of the icing with red food colouring and cover with cling film. Colour the remaining icing with green food colouring.

★ Place house on cake board and cover it with green icing, reserving a little for later. Place red icing in a plastic piping bag with a star nozzle and pipe the roof, or just use a fork to mark the tiles. Attach the chimney and coat with red icing, too.

★ Dust a worktop with icing sugar and roll out a little white sugar paste. Cut out shapes to make the windows and press on to the cake, and cut out a path and attach to the board. Mix some blue colouring into a little sugar paste, roll out and make the shutters and door.

★ Using the sugar paste and food colourings, cut out small blossoms and press on to the cake. Colour the remaining green icing a shade darker and place into a piping bag, snip off the end and pipe leaves and trailing stems over the cake. Use a little red butter cream to pipe foxgloves or little flowers, if you like.

★ Colour the desiccated coconut with a little green food colouring and scatter over the cake board, adding a few flowers, if you like.

RECIPE, FOOD AND PROP STYLING: MITZIE WILSON **PHOTO:** CLARE WINFIELD

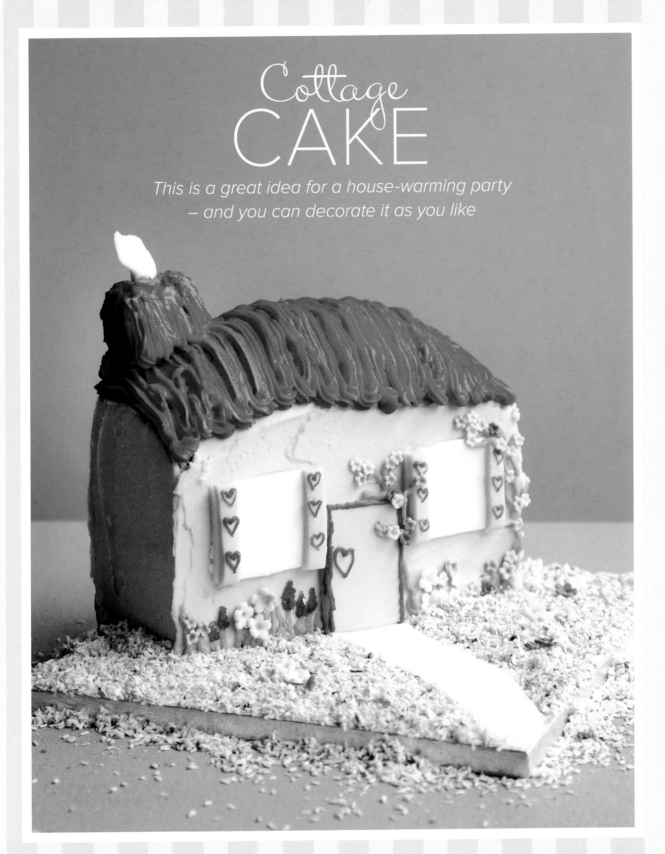

Cottage CAKE

This is a great idea for a house-warming party
– and you can decorate it as you like

Celebration CAKE

A glorious two-tier confection of lemon sponge, carrot cake and cream cheese icing

Try this
Both cakes will keep in the freezer for up to 3 months. Defrost overnight before icing.

SERVES 30 **PREP** 1 HR 30 MINS, PLUS CHILLING **BAKE** 1 HR 35 MINS

FOR THE LEMON SPONGE

- 250g butter at room temperature
- 300g caster sugar
- 5 medium eggs, beaten
- 350g plain flour
- 3tsp baking powder
- 5-6tbsp lemon juice
- Zest of 3 lemons
- 3tbsp lemon curd

FOR THE CARROT CAKE

- 220ml sunflower oil
- 4 medium eggs
- 175g self-raising flour
- 175g self-raising wholemeal flour
- 175g light muscovado sugar
- 1tsp ground cinnamon
- 175g carrots, coarsely grated
- Zest and juice of 1 large orange
- 125g raisins

FOR THE ICING

- 400g icing sugar
- 200g soft butter
- 1tbsp vanilla extract
- 600g full-fat cream cheese

YOU WILL NEED

- A 25cm round cake tin and a 20cm round cake tin, both greased and lined with baking parchment
- A 30cm cake board or cake stand
- A thin 20cm cake board
- A sugar flower, to decorate (optional)

★ Preheat oven to gas mark 4/180°C (160°C in a fan oven).

★ **TO MAKE LEMON SPONGE,** beat butter and sugar until fluffy. Gradually beat in eggs. Fold in flour, baking powder, lemon juice and zest. Add mixture to larger tin, spreading it out.

★ Bake for 45 mins or until firm in centre. Allow to cool for 10 mins, then turn out on to a wire rack to cool completely. When cold, trim the top so that it is flat, then cut in half horizontally and sandwich together again with lemon curd.

★ **TO MAKE CARROT CAKE,** beat together oil and eggs. Add flours, sugar, cinnamon, carrots, orange zest and juice and raisins to a large bowl. Add egg mixture and stir well. Spoon mixture into smaller cake tin and bake for 45-50 mins or until it has risen, is golden and bounces back when pressed lightly in the middle. Leave to cool for 5 mins, then transfer to a wire rack to cool completely. Trim the top so it is flat.

★ **TO MAKE ICING,** sift icing sugar into a large bowl, then add butter and vanilla. Beat with an electric whisk on low, then add cream cheese and stir until just combined.

★ Place both cakes on cake boards and cover the tops and sides with icing. If very crumbly, cover with a thin coat, chill, then repeat with a second coat of icing. Place carrot cake on top of lemon cake and add a little more icing to cover the join. (Keep the cakes on the boards, as it makes it easier to remove a tier and cut it later.) Keep cake chilled for up to 24 hrs before serving.

★ **PERFECT FINISH** To decorate your cake, you can buy large, handmade sugar flowers online, such as this peony, or ask a local cake decorator to make one for you. You could also use a silk or fresh flower.

RECIPES, FOOD STYLING AND PROP STYLING: MITZIE WILSON **PHOTO:** KATIE WILSON

SERVES 16 PREP 1 HR, PLUS SETTING BAKE 1 HR

FOR THE CAKE
- 150g butter, at room temperature
- 200g caster sugar
- 3 medium eggs (at room temperature), beaten
- 225g plain flour
- 1½tsp baking powder
- Zest of 1 lemon and 3tbsp lemon juice
- 4tbsp lemon curd

FOR THE ICING
- 200g butter, softened
- 400g icing sugar
- Drop of vanilla extract

FOR THE BISCUITS
- Zest of ½ lemon and 1tbsp lemon juice
- 100g butter
- 100g caster sugar
- 175g plain flour, plus extra for dusting
- 1 egg yolk
- 250g royal icing sugar
- Pink food colouring
- Coloured sugar strands
- Pink sugar bonbons

YOU WILL NEED
- A 20.5cm round, deep cake tin, greased and lined with baking parchment,
- A bunny biscuit cutter (about 9cm tall)
- 2 baking trays
- 2 piping bags
- A fine piping nozzle

★ Preheat oven to gas mark 4/180°C (160°C in a fan oven). To make the cake, beat butter and sugar together until light and fluffy. Add eggs, a little at a time, beating well. Add a little flour if the mixture begins to curdle. Beat in the remaining flour and the baking powder, lemon zest and lemon juice.

★ Place mixture in cake tin and bake for 35-45 mins or until a skewer comes out clean when inserted in the centre and the cake is firm and a golden colour. Allow to cool for 10 mins, then turn out on to a wire rack and leave to cool completely.

★ Cut cake in half horizontally. Spread lemon curd over the bottom half, then add the top half of the cake.

★ **TO MAKE ICING,** mix butter, icing sugar and vanilla with a little boiling water and beat until smooth and creamy. Spread generously over the top and sides of cake.

★ **TO MAKE BISCUITS,** place zest, butter, sugar and flour in a food processor and blend until fine crumbs. Add egg yolk and 1-2tsp lemon juice. Blend for a few secs, adding more lemon juice, if needed, until it forms a ball. Chill dough for at least 15 mins.

★ Roll out dough on a lightly floured work surface to the thickness of a £1 coin. Cut out bunny shapes with a cutter and place on baking tray. Bake for 10-12 mins until golden at the edges. Leave to cool for 10 mins, then remove from tray and leave to cool completely.

★ Mix royal icing sugar with water according to pack instructions. Add food colouring until desired shade. Place a third of the icing in a piping bag fitted with a fine nozzle and pipe an outline around each biscuit.

★ Mix remaining icing with a little water until the consistency of thick pouring cream. Place in a second piping bag, snip off the end, then pipe icing inside the border (to fill it). Add a bonbon to each, as a tail.

★ Allow biscuits to set for 2 to 3 hrs and store in a cake tin until needed. Arrange around the outside of the cake. Sprinkle sugar strands over the top of the cake and add a few bonbons.

★ The cake will keep for 3 to 4 days in an airtight container.

RECIPE, FOOD AND PROP STYLING: MITZIE WILSON PHOTO: TOBY SCOTT

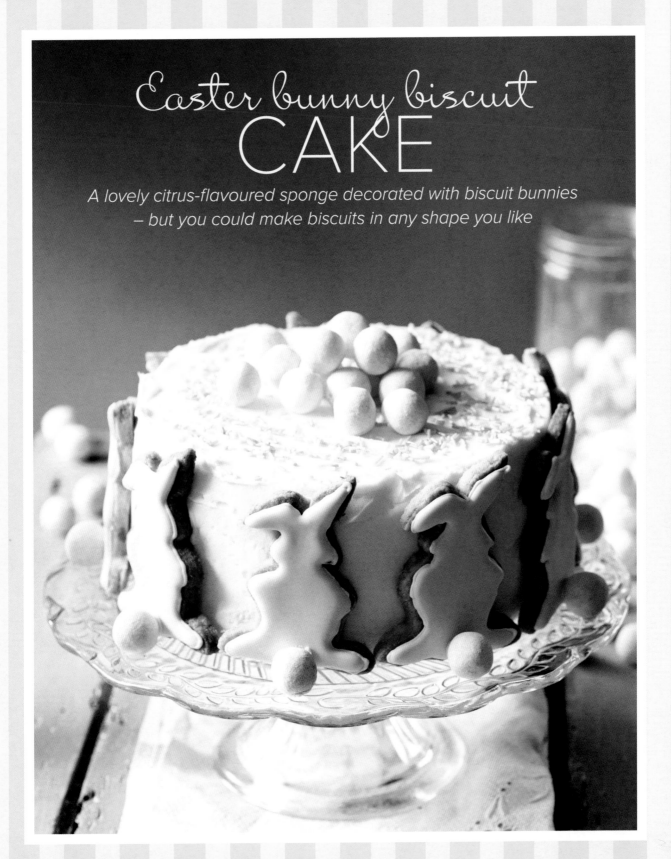

Easter bunny biscuit CAKE

A lovely citrus-flavoured sponge decorated with biscuit bunnies – but you could make biscuits in any shape you like

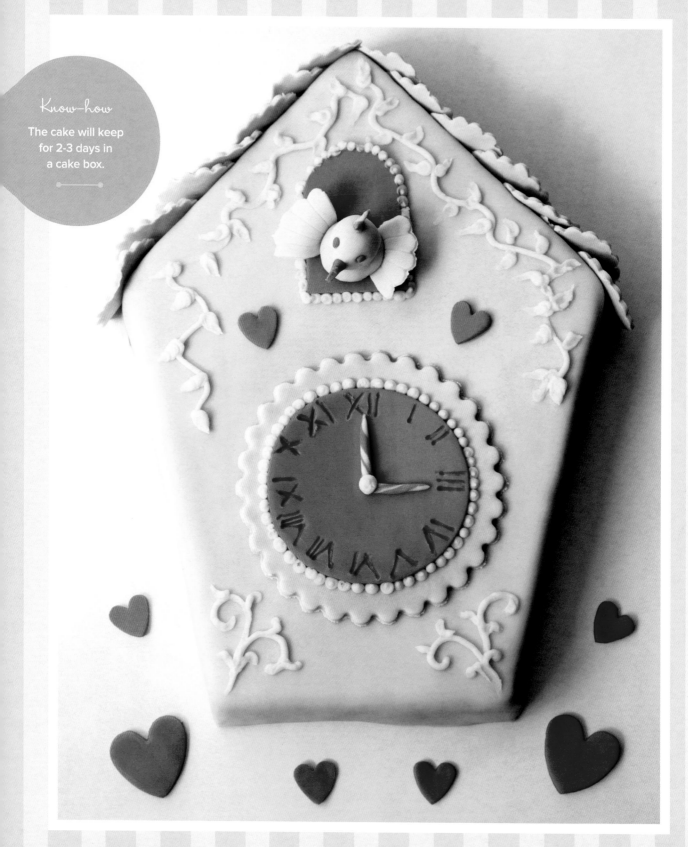

Know-how
The cake will keep for 2-3 days in a cake box.

Cuckoo clock
CAKE

This cake is perfect for any celebration and the decoration is easily made with biscuit cutters

SERVES 12 **PREP** 1 HR 30 MINS **BAKE** 40 MINS

RECIPE, FOOD AND PROP STYLING: MITZIE WILSON **PHOTO:** CLARE WINFIELD

FOR THE SPONGE
- 225g softened butter or baking spread
- 225g caster sugar
- 275g self-raising flour
- 2tsp baking powder
- 4 large eggs
- 2tsp vanilla extract

FOR THE ICING
- 4tbsp seedless raspberry jam
- 500g blue sugar paste
- 100g purple sugar paste
- 100g bright pink sugar paste
- 50g butter
- 150g icing sugar, sifted, plus extra for dusting
- A little green food colouring

YOU WILL NEED
- A 23cm x 33cm tray bake tin, greased and base lined with baking parchment
- A 24cm x 35 cm cake board
- A 4cm round fluted cutter
- A paintbrush
- A 8cm round fluted cutter
- A 7cm plain cutter
- A small (1cm) heart cutter
- A piping bag

★ Preheat oven to gas mark 4/180°C (160°C in a fan oven).

★ **TO MAKE THE SPONGE** Add all the ingredients to a bowl and beat with a wooden spoon until blended. Place mixture in the tin and level the top.

★ Bake for 35-40 mins or until cake has shrunk away from the sides of the tin. Leave to cool in the tin for 10 mins, then turn out, remove baking parchment and allow to cool completely.

★ **TO DECORATE,** cut cake in half horizontally. Spread half of the jam over 1 half, then top with other cake half. Cut out a clock shape; discard trimmings. Place cake on cake board. Spread rest of jam over the top and sides.

★ Dust a work top with icing sugar, then roll out blue icing thinly until it's large enough to cover the cake. Drape over the cake and trim. Re-roll trimmings and cover with cling film.

★ **TO MAKE ROOF TILES,** roll out purple icing and cut out circles with a 4cm cutter. Brush each with a paint brush slightly dampened with water – so they stick to the cake and each other – and overlap them across the roof. Use a 8cm cutter and cut out the base of the clock dial. Brush with a damp paintbrush and place on the cake.

★ Roll out pink sugar paste, cut out a 7cm circle with a cutter and arrange on top of the dial. Mark numerals with a cocktail stick. Cut out a small door and place above clock dial. Cut out a few hearts and secure to the cake. Roll out small pieces of pink and white sugar paste into thin sausages, then twist together and shape into clock hands and some bird 'feathers' (for its head).

★ Mix together butter, icing sugar and green food colouring, then place in a piping bag and snip off the end. Pipe dots on to the dial and around the door, then pipe leaf decorations.

★ Shape blue sugar paste into a bird and add a pink beak and eyes. Secure all decorations by brushing the backs with a damp paintbrush and press on to cake.

Daisy CAKE

*This grown-up birthday cake uses vanilla sponge,
but works equally well with chocolate cake*

SERVES 12 **PREP** 1 HR 30 MINS, PLUS CHILLING **BAKE** 45 MINS

FOR THE SPONGE
- 400g butter, softened
- 400g caster sugar
- 1tsp vanilla extract
- 8 medium eggs, beaten
- 400g self-raising flour
- 1tsp baking powder
- 4tbsp raspberry jam

FOR THE ICING
- 50g butter
- 150g icing sugar, plus extra for dusting
- ½tsp vanilla extract
- 1kg yellow sugar paste
- 50g each pink, orange and purple sugar paste

YOU WILL NEED
- 2 x 20cm round, deep cake tins, greased and lined with baking parchment
- A 25cm round cake board
- Large and small gerbera or daisy plunger cutters
- A Medium blossom plunger cutters
- A paintbrush
- Birthday candles
- A 50cm yellow ribbon

★ Preheat oven to gas mark 4/180°C (160° in a fan oven).

★ **TO MAKE THE SPONGE**
Place butter, sugar and vanilla in a bowl and beat with a wooden spoon or electric whisk until the butter has become a pale colour and the mixture is light and fluffy. Add eggs, a little at a time, beating after each addition.

★ Sift together flour and baking powder. Add 1-2tbsp flour to egg mixture to prevent it curdling, if necessary, then fold in remaining flour with a large metal spoon. Divide mixture between tins.

★ Bake for 35-45 mins. Cakes should be firm in the centre and a skewer should come out clean when inserted in the centre. If it doesn't, bake for a little longer. Allow to cool in the tins for 10 mins, then turn out cakes and leave to cool completely.

★ Trim the top of the cakes so they are level. Sandwich cakes together with jam and place on a cake board.

★ **TO MAKE ICING**, beat together butter, icing sugar and vanilla to make a smooth icing, then spread this thinly and smoothly all over the cake. Put in the fridge to chill.

★ Roll out the yellow sugar paste on a worktop lightly dusted with icing sugar to a circle large enough to cover the top and sides of the cake generously. Drape over the cake and smooth on to the sides, using your palms. Trim off any excess. Re-roll sugar paste trimmings thinly and cut out a few small blossoms.

★ Roll out the other coloured icings, one at a time, and cut out flowers. Brush each with a paintbrush, slightly dampened with water, and position them on the cake. Add candles and use ribbon to trim the board.

★ **TO MAKE CHOCOLATE CAKE**, reduce the quantity of flour by 100g and use 100g cocoa powder instead with an extra ½tsp baking powder.

RECIPE, FOOD AND PROP STYLING: MITZIE WILSON **PHOTO:** CLARE WINFIELD

Cute kitty CAKE

We used a rich chocolate mixture as the base for this cake. Decorate it with icings coloured to match the colour of your cat

SERVES 8 **PREP** 1 HR **BAKE** 30 MINS

FOR THE CHOCOLATE CAKE

- 100g butter
- 100g light muscovado sugar
- 100g plain chocolate
- 50ml soured cream
- 1 egg
- 100g self-raising flour
- 2 tbsp cocoa powder

FOR THE ICING

- 100g butter
- 200g icing sugar

TO DECORATE

- 50g chocolate flavour sugar paste
- 50g white sugar paste
- Blue and pink concentrated paste food colourings
- A few strands of spaghetti (for whiskers)
- Sugar mice (optional)

YOU WILL NEED

- A 20.5cm round cake tin, base lined with baking parchment
- A piping bag with a small star nozzle

★ Preheat oven to gas mark 4/180°C (160°C in a fan oven).

★ Heat butter, sugar and 50ml hot water in a medium pan until melted. Add chocolate and stir until melted. Leave to cool for 1-2 mins. Beat in soured cream, then egg. Add flour and cocoa powder and mix well until smooth. Add to cake tin and bake for 25-30 mins or until mixture feels just firm in the centre. Allow to cool in the tin for 10 mins, then turn out and allow to cool completely.

★ **TO MAKE ICING** Meanwhile, beat butter and icing sugar together until smooth, then place in a piping bag fitted with a small star nozzle. Pipe stars all over the top of the cold cake.

★ **TO DECORATE** Shape ears and cheeks from the chocolate sugar paste and place on the cake, piping icing inside the ears for detail. Colour a little sugar paste blue and cut out 2 oval eyes, then top with circles of chocolate sugar paste, and pipe small white dots for pupils. Colour a very small piece of sugar paste pink, then shape into a heart-shaped nose and add to the cake. Stick the spaghetti strands into the 'cheeks' for whiskers.

RECIPE, FOOD AND PROP STYLING: MITZIE WILSON **PHOTO:** TOBY SCOTT

SERVES 8 PREP 2 HRS, PLUS SETTING BAKE 25 MINS

FOR THE DECORATIONS
- 250g pack sugar paste
- Pink, lilac and green paste food colourings
- Pink and violet edible lustre

FOR THE SPONGE
- 200g butter
- 200g caster sugar
- 4 medium eggs, beaten
- 200g self-raising flour
- ½tsp vanilla extract

FOR THE VANILLA SYRUP
- 50g caster sugar
- ½tsp vanilla extract

FOR THE ICING
- 200g butter, softened
- 400g icing sugar, plus extra for dusting
- 1tsp vanilla extract
- 4tbsp raspberry jam

YOU WILL NEED
- A hydrangea cutter and mould; veined rose leaf plunger cutter and veined butterfly plunger cutter (from cake shops)
- 3 x 15cm round sponge tins, greased and base lined with baking parchment
- A paintbrush

★ **FOR THE DECORATIONS**
It's best to make these a day in advance. Set aside a quarter of the white sugar paste to make leaves. Divide remaining sugar paste in half and colour with pink and lilac paste colours – you can make varying shades if you like. Colour reserved sugar paste with green colouring to make the leaves. Keep all sugar paste covered with cling film to prevent it drying out.

★ Roll out sugar paste, 1 piece at a time, on a worktop lightly dusted with icing sugar. Using cutters, cut out flowers, leaves and butterflies as directed on pack instructions, pressing down on the mould or veiner moulds to give an embossed pattern. Leave to dry on crumpled kitchen paper for at least 1 day (they will keep for up to 3 months in an airtight container).

★ Preheat oven to gas mark 4/180°C (160°C in a fan oven).

★ **TO MAKE THE SPONGE**
Place butter and sugar in a bowl and beat with a wooden spoon or electric whisk until butter becomes a pale colour and mixture is light and fluffy.

★ Add eggs, a little at a time, beating well after each addition. Add 1-2tbsp flour to prevent mixture curdling, if necessary, then fold in the rest of the flour with a large metal spoon. Add vanilla extract and stir in.

★ Divide mixture equally between tins and bake for 20-25 mins until golden brown and just firm to the touch. Remove from tins and allow to cool completely on a wire rack.

★ To make syrup, place sugar in a pan with 100ml water and boil for 3-4 mins until sugar has dissolved. Add vanilla, leave to cool, then drizzle over cakes.

★ **TO MAKE ICING,** whisk or beat together butter, sugar and vanilla with 1-2tsp boiling water until light and creamy.

★ Spread 2 cakes with jam, place on top of each other, then top with the third cake. Place on a small plate. Cover all over with a thin layer of icing. Chill in fridge until firm, then coat with a second layer of icing, making a slight dome shape on the top to give a little height.

★ Using a fine paint brush, dust petals and leaves with edible lustres, then use to decorate cake as desired.

RECIPE, FOOD AND PROP STYLING: MITZIE WILSON PHOTO: TOBY SCOTT

Hydrangea CAKE

We baked the mixture in three cake tins, but if you only have two,
bake the mixture for the third layer once the others come out the oven

Try this

To give the cake extra height, place it on top of a 15cm drum cake board and ice over the sides.

Lace-trimmed CAKE

This cake uses a silicone mould to make the lace, giving a stunning, professional-looking finish

SERVES 30 **PREP** 3 HRS, PLUS DRYING **BAKE** 20 MINS (FOR THE LACE)

FOR THE CAKE
- 18cm and 23cm round deep fruit cakes or Madeira cakes

FOR THE ICING
- 1.575kg almond paste, plus extra to secure cakes
- Apricot jam, warmed
- Icing sugar, for dusting
- 1.575kg white sugar paste

FOR THE LACE
- 100g Magic Icing Powder (available from Lakeland)
- Blue food colouring
- Silver shimmer spray (we used Dr Oetker)
- A few royal icing sugar blossoms

YOU WILL NEED
- A 50cm pink ric rac ribbon
- A 18cm round thin cake board
- A 30cm round drum cake board
- 4 plastic cake dowels
- 1 small and 1 large Lace-Look Silicone Icing Mat (from lakeland.co.uk)

RECIPE, FOOD AND PROP STYLING: MITZIE WILSON **PHOTO:** CLARE WINFIELD

★ Trim the top of the cakes so they are level. Place small cake on a thin cake board and large cake on a large drum board, sticking in place with a little ball of almond paste. Brush jam all over the cakes.

★ Roll out 675g almond paste into a circle large enough to cover the top and side of small cake. Drape over cake, easing out any pleats and using your palms to smooth almond paste evenly against the cake. Trim off any excess. Repeat process with larger cake, using 900g almond paste. Leave cakes to dry for 2-3 days.

★ Brush boiled water very lightly over the almond paste – do not make the paste wet or sticky.

★ Roll out 675g sugar paste into a circle large enough to cover the top and sides of the small cake, then drape over the cake, easing out any pleats on the side and using your palms to smooth the icing evenly against the cake. Lift the skirt of the icing to ease out any pleats and use the side of your hand to smooth the icing against the cake. Trim off any excess. Repeat process with the larger cake, using 900g sugar paste.

★ **TO MAKE LACE,** mix Magic Icing with water according to the pack instructions. Add a little food colouring to give the desired shade. Spread Magic Icing over the small silicone mat as directed on the pack. Make sure you scrape off all excess icing to make the lace clean and sharp. Bake at gas mark ½/130°C (110°C in a fan oven) for 6 mins or as directed on the pack, then peel away icing. Repeat process to make 3 strips of lace icing. Use Magic Icing to cover a large silicone lace mat and peel away individual lace doilies. Repeat process once more. Place lace pieces between sheets of baking parchment and cover with cling film. They will stay flexible for 3-4 days.

★ **TO DECORATE CAKE,** trim dowels so they are the same height as the large cake (and fit flush with the top). Insert into the centre of the large cake, spaced well apart, and place small cake on top. The dowels will stop the cake sinking.

★ Spray cake with shimmer spray. Using a damp paint brush, paint the back of the lace strips with water and wrap 2 around the base of large cake, so they overlap on the board. Attach small doilies to the small cake in the same way.

★ Cut off the lace edge of the last strip of icing and attach to the top edge of the smaller cake. Snip the individual lace flowers out of the strip and place on top of the cake.

★ Fold 4 or 5 doilies in half and half again, then arrange on top of the cake to make a centrepiece, using a little water to help them stick together. Dampen the back of icing blossoms and press on to the cake. Attach ribbon to the board.

Mini meringue
MOUTHFULS

Pastel meringues will look lovely as part of a celebratory afternoon tea

MAKES 20 PAIRS **PREP** 20 MINS **BAKE** 1 HR 30 MINS

FOR THE MERINGUES
- 2 egg whites
- 100g caster sugar
- Pink, yellow, green and lilac food colouring, as desired
- 15ml double cream, whipped

YOU WILL NEED
- A large plastic piping bag and a 2cm star nozzle
- 2 baking sheets, lined with baking parchment
- Small paper cases

★ Preheat oven to gas mark ¼/110°C (90°C in a fan oven).

★ **TO MAKE MERINGUES,** place egg whites and sugar in a bowl and whisk with an electric mixer for 10 mins until meringue is smooth, glossy and can stand in firm peaks. A stand mixer is best – just set the timer and leave it to do its work.

★ Divide meringue mixture between 4 bowls and add a drop of different food colouring to each, stirring until the colour is even throughout.

★ Place one batch of mixture in a piping bag and pipe small rounds on to the baking sheets. Wash the bag and repeat with the remaining colours. Bake meringues for 1 hr-1 hr 30 mins or until they are dry and firm and come off the baking parchment easily. Turn off the oven and leave meringues inside to dry a little longer, if you like.

★ Whip cream until it holds its shape, then use to sandwich the meringues together in pairs. Place in the paper cases and serve within 2 hrs. Unfilled, they will keep for 1 week in a cake tin.

RECIPE, FOOD AND PROP STYLING: MITZIE WILSON PHOTO: CLARE WINFIELD

Try this
If you don't have a piping bag, use a teaspoon to get the right-sized dollop of meringue mixture.

Pistachio, lime + rose
ICED LOAF

This is a lovely, fragrant cake that has a delicate hint of rose water

SERVES 12 **PREP** 35 MINS **BAKE** 1 HR

RECIPE AND FOOD STYLING: MITZIE WILSON PROP STYLING: SUE ROWLANDS PHOTO: TOBY SCOTT

FOR THE SPONGE
- 200g butter, at room temperature
- 200g caster sugar
- 4 medium eggs, beaten
- 200g self-raising flour
- ½tsp baking powder
- 2 limes
- 50g shelled pistachios, finely chopped, plus extra halves, to decorate
- ½tsp rose extract (we used Nielsen-Massey)

TO DECORATE
- 200g fondant icing sugar
- Juice and zest of 1 lime
- A few rose petals

YOU WILL NEED
- A 900g loaf tin, lined with baking parchment

★ Preheat oven to gas mark 3/170°C (150°C in a fan oven). Place butter and sugar in a bowl and beat until light and creamy. Gradually beat in eggs, adding a little flour if mixture curdles.

★ Add the remaining flour and the baking powder, lime zest, 2tbsp lime juice, most of the pistachios and the rose extract. Fold in until well mixed.

★ Spread mixture evenly in tin and bake for 55-60 mins until it has risen, is golden brown and a skewer comes out clean when inserted in the centre. Allow to cool in tin for 10 mins, then turn out and allow to cool completely. Remove baking parchment and place loaf upside down on a cake plate.

★ **TO DECORATE,** mix fondant icing sugar with just enough lime juice to make a thick pouring consistency, then drizzle over loaf. Scatter over lime zest, the pistachio halves and the rose petals. Serve in slices.

Rainbow meringue
LAYERS

Serve this stack of meringues with a compote
of mixed berries for an impressive dessert

SERVES 8-10 **PREP** 1 HR **BAKE** 2 HRS

FOR THE MERINGUE
- 6 egg whites, at room temperature
- 300g caster sugar
- Gel food colours in various shades

FOR THE FILLING
- 300ml double cream
- Sugar sprinkles

YOU WILL NEED
- 2 baking trays, lined with baking parchment

★ Preheat oven to gas mark ½/130°C (110°C in a fan oven).

★ Draw a circle about 18cm in diameter on each sheet of baking parchment.

★ **TO MAKE MERINGUES,** prepare the first batch by using half the ingredients. Put 3 egg whites in a large, clean bowl and beat them with an electric whisk or mixer at a slow speed. Once they are looking frothy, increase the speed to medium and whisk until they stand in stiff peaks.

★ Whisk in 150g sugar, 1tbsp at a time, on high speed until you have a stiff, glossy meringue.

★ Divide mixture in half and colour each half with a little different food colouring. Using a teaspoon, drop 3 or 4 small blobs of each meringue on to the trays (outside the circle), and spread the rest of each mixture within the circles.

★ Put the meringues in the oven and bake for 1 hr. Turn off the oven and leave meringues inside to cool, then carefully remove from the trays, keeping them on the baking parchment.

★ Add extra baking parchment to the trays and repeat process to prepare second set of meringues. When ready to serve, whip cream until it just forms soft peaks. Carefully remove baking parchment from meringues and lay 1 on a plate. Spread over some whipped cream and stack another meringue on top – repeat until all meringue layers have been used. Dip the bottoms of each mini meringue first in cream, then sprinkles and place on top of the meringue pile. Serve within 1 hr.

★ The unfilled meringues will keep for 1 week in a cake tin.

RECIPE, FOOD AND PROP STYLING: MITZIE WILSON **PHOTO:** TOBY SCOTT

Try this
The meringues are best made in 2 batches, unless you have a double oven.

Know-how

Applying a thin layer of icing first – a crumb coat – helps to seal in the crumbs.

Raspberry layer CAKE

This ombre cake is perfect for a summer get-together

SERVES 10   **PREP** 2 HRS, PLUS CHILLING   **BAKE** 25 MINS

RECIPE, FOOD AND PROP STYLING: MITZIE WILSON **PHOTO:** CLARE WINFIELD

FOR THE SPONGE
- 250g butter
- 250g caster sugar
- 5 medium eggs, beaten
- 250g self-raising flour
- 1tsp natural raspberry flavouring (available from Lakeland)
- Pink food colouring
- 4tbsp raspberry jam
- 200g raspberries

FOR THE ICING
- 300g icing sugar
- 150g butter, softened
- 1tbsp vanilla extract
- 400g full-fat cream cheese
- A few drops of natural raspberry flavouring (optional)

YOU WILL NEED
- 4 x 18cm round sponge tins, greased and lined with baking parchment

★ Preheat oven to gas mark 4/180˚C (160˚C in a fan oven).

★ **TO MAKE THE SPONGE,** place butter and sugar in a mixing bowl and beat until light and fluffy. Gradually beat in eggs until mixture is smooth and light, then fold in flour and raspberry flavouring.

★ Divide mixture equally between 4 small bowls. Add a little pink food colouring to each, varying the shades, so they go from a pale to deep colour. (It's best to first mix a small amount of cake mixture from one bowl with the food colouring, then evenly stir it into the rest of the mixture in that bowl.) Add each batch of mixture to a cake tin, spread out, and bake for 20-25 mins until firm to the touch and a golden brown colour.

★ **FOR THE ICING** Meanwhile, sift icing sugar into a large bowl and add butter and vanilla. Use an electric whisk on low speed and beat until it is well mixed. Add cream cheese and stir until just combined. Add a drop of food colouring and a few drops of raspberry flavouring (to taste), if you like.

★ Sandwich cakes together using jam, with the darkest sponge at the bottom and the palest on top. Place on a cake board and cover completely with a thin layer of icing. Chill for 15 mins, then repeat with a thicker layer of icing. Keep cake chilled until ready to serve, then move to a cake stand and top with raspberries.

Raspberry, redcurrant + rose SPONGE

Whether for a birthday or thank you, treat a friend to this beautiful cake, which is a light as a feather – and contains no butter

SERVES 8 **PREP** 30 MINS **BAKE** 20 MINS

FOR THE SPONGE
- 3 medium eggs
- 75g caster sugar
- 75g plain flour
- ½tsp baking powder

FOR THE FILLING
- 150ml double cream
- 1tbsp icing sugar, plus extra for dusting
- 300g mixed berries

FOR CRYSTALLISED ROSES
- 1 egg white
- 3 roses, stems removed
- 2tbsp caster sugar

YOU WILL NEED
- 2 x 20.5cm sandwich cake tins, greased and lined with baking parchment
- A paintbrush

★ Preheat oven to gas mark 5/190°C (170°C in a fan oven).

★ **FOR THE SPONGE** Using an electric stand mixer, whisk together eggs and sugar for 2 mins. Add 75ml warm water, then whisk for about 10 mins until mixture is thick, mousse-like and has trebled in volume – it should leave a trail when the whisk is lifted. (Or use an electric hand whisk in a bowl set over hot water.)

★ Sift flour and baking powder together, then carefully fold into egg mixture, using a large metal spoon. Be very careful not to knock out the air and make sure that there are no pockets of flour.

★ Divide mixture between tins and bake for 20 mins until golden brown and just shrinking away from the sides of the tin. Leave to cool for 5 mins, then turn out cakes on to a wire rack, flip over again, and leave them to cool completely.

★ **FOR THE FILLING,** whip cream with icing sugar until thick, then spread over 1 cake. Top with fruit, retaining a few berries for decoration. Place second cake on top and dust with icing sugar.

★ **FOR THE CRYSTALLISED ROSES,** whisk egg white with a fork. Paint rose petals with egg white, then sprinkle over caster sugar. Leave on baking parchment to dry, preferably overnight. Arrange on top of the cake with the remaining berries. (Once cake has been filled, serve within a couple of hours.)

RECIPE, FOOD AND PROP STYLING: MITZIE WILSON **PHOTO:** TOBY SCOTT

Ruffle CAKE

This celebration cake is made with sponge soaked in vanilla syrup,
but you could use lemon, coffee or chocolate flavours, too

SERVES 12 **PREP** 2 HRS, PLUS CHILLING **BAKE** 25 MINS

RECIPE, FOOD AND PROP STYLING: MITZIE WILSON **PHOTO:** TOBY SCOTT

FOR THE SPONGE
- 250g butter, softened
- 250g caster sugar
- 5 medium eggs, beaten
- 250g self-raising flour
- 1tsp vanilla extract

FOR THE SUGAR SYRUP
- 150ml water
- 150ml caster sugar
- ½tsp vanilla extract

TO DECORATE
- 6 large egg whites
- 500g caster sugar
- ½tsp vanilla extract
- 600g butter, softened and cut into cubes
- Food colouring
- 4tbsp raspberry jam

YOU WILL NEED
- 4 x 15cm round sponge tins (or bake in 2 batches)
- A large piping bag
- A tear-shaped nozzle (Jem petal tip, no 104)

★ Preheat oven to gas mark 4/180°C (160°C in a fan oven).

★ **TO MAKE SPONGE**, place butter and sugar in a mixing bowl and beat until light and fluffy. Gradually beat in eggs until mixture is smooth and light. Fold in flour with vanilla. Divide the mixture equally between 4 tins (or make 2 cakes at a time).

★ Bake cakes for 20-25 mins until golden brown and firm to the touch.

★ To make sugar syrup, place water in a small pan with sugar and vanilla and bring to the boil, then simmer for 5 mins. Pour over hot cakes, then leave them to cool before turning out.

★ **TO DECORATE** The cake is iced with Swiss meringue buttercream. Place egg whites in a large bowl over a pan of gently simmering water. Add sugar and stir until it has dissolved. Remove from the heat and transfer mixture to an electric stand mixer. Whisk until it forms stiff peaks like a meringue.

★ Add vanilla and butter, 1 cube at a time, whisking at full speed until combined, and mixture is smooth, thick and creamy. If it doesn't seem to thicken or appears curdled, keep whisking until it cools. Add food colouring, as desired.

★ Sandwich cakes – one on top of the other – with raspberry jam. Place cake on a plate and cover all over with a thin layer of icing. Leave to chill in the fridge for 15 mins.

★ Place icing in a piping bag fitted with a petal nozzle. Holding the nozzle with the wide end of the tip against the side of the cake, and using a backwards and forwards movement, pipe icing in 2-3cm strips up the sides of the cake. Pipe a ruffle on the top, around the edge, to finish.

★ The cake is best kept chilled until ready to serve.

Individual iced CAKES

Serve everyone their own little cake – and decorate it to suit the person

MAKES 4 CAKES **PREP** 2 HRS, PLUS SETTING **BAKE** 45 MINS

FOR THE CAKES
- 150g butter at room temperature
- 200g caster sugar
- 1tsp vanilla extract
- 3 medium eggs (at room temperature), beaten
- 225g plain flour
- 1½tsp baking powder
- Zest and juice of 2 lemons
- 50g caster sugar
- 4tbsp raspberry jam

FOR THE ICING
- 75g butter, softened
- 250g icing sugar, plus extra for dusting

TO DECORATE
- 500g ready-to-roll sugar paste
- A little green concentrated paste food colourings
- Edible shimmer balls
- White piping icing or royal icing
- Ribbon or lace

YOU WILL NEED
- A 20.5cm square cake tin, lined with baking parchment
- A 8cm round cutter and string
- 4 small circles of card

★ Preheat oven to gas mark 4/180°C (160°C in a fan oven).

★ **TO MAKE CAKES**, place butter, 200g caster sugar and vanilla extract in a bowl and beat with an electric mixer until light and fluffy. Gradually beat in eggs, a little at a time, until mixture is smooth and light.

★ Sift together flour and baking power, then beat half of it into cake mixture. Carefully beat in the remaining flour, plus the zest and 3tbsp lemon juice until mixture is light and well mixed.

★ Place in cake tin and bake for 35-45 mins until firm and a skewer inserted in the middle comes out clean. Allow to cool in tin for 10 mins, then turn out and allow to cool completely.

★ To make syrup, place 50g sugar in a small pan with the remaining lemon juice and 2tbsp water. Simmer until sugar has dissolved.

★ **TO MAKE ICING**, beat together butter and sugar with 1tsp boiling water.

★ Cut cake in half horizontally, then brush each half with a little syrup and sandwich them together again with jam and a little icing. Using the cutter, cut out 4 small cakes.

★ Cover cakes with a thin layer of icing, then chill for a few minutes to set. Smooth the icing, then spread over a second layer of icing.

★ Use a piece of string to measure the top and side of a cake and add on a further 4cm – use this as the width of your icing circles.

★ Colour icing pale green, then cut into quarters. Roll out 1 piece at a time on a worktop dusted with icing sugar until the width of the string. Drape 1 piece of icing over 1 cake and smooth against the sides, easing out any pleats. Place cake on card and wrap ribbon around the base. Pipe 4 heart shapes in a circle on top of each cake to form a flower, then decorate with shimmer balls.

RECIPE, FOOD AND PROP STYLING: MITZIE WILSON PHOTO: DAN JONES

Know-how
These cakes will keep
for up to 1 week
in a cake tin.

Try this
Store the blossoms and butterflies in an airtight container – they'll keep for months.

Blossom + butterfly CAKE

Turn a simple Victoria sponge into something special with some clever decorating ideas

SERVES 12 **PREP** 20 MINS, PLUS CHILLING **BAKE** 30 MINS

RECIPE AND FOOD STYLING: MITZIE WILSON PROP STYLING: SUE ROWLANDS PHOTO: TOBY SCOTT

FOR THE SPONGE
- 375g butter, softened
- 375g light muscovado sugar
- 7 large eggs, beaten
- 375g self-raising flour
- 1tsp baking powder
- 6tsp raspberry jam or lemon curd

TO DECORATE
- 250g softened butter
- 600g icing sugar, plus extra for dusting
- Green, yellow, pink and lilac concentrated paste food colours
- 250g sugar paste

YOU WILL NEED
- 3 x 20.5cm round sponge tins, greased and base lined with baking parchment
- A drum cake board
- Blossom and butterfly cutters
- Pink and lilac edible lustre
- A large piping bag

★ Preheat oven to gas mark 4/180°C (160°C in a fan oven).

★ **TO MAKE THE SPONGE,** place butter and sugar in a mixing bowl and beat until really light and fluffy. Gradually beat in eggs, a little at a time, adding a little flour if mixture begins to curdle. Fold in the rest of the flour and the baking powder until evenly mixed.

★ Divide mixture evenly between tins and bake for 25-30 mins until just firm in the centre. Leave to cool in tins for 5 mins, then turn out and leave to cool completely on a wire rack. Sandwich cakes together with jam or lemon curd and place on a cake board.

★ **TO MAKE ICING,** mix butter and icing sugar with a little boiling water until smooth and creamy. Place about 6tbsp in a small bowl and mix in green food colouring to desired shade. Cover and set aside.

★ Spread a little icing thinly all over the cake to seal in the crumbs. Place in fridge to chill for 10 mins, then cover with a thicker layer of icing.

★ Spread green icing over the board and 1cm up the base of the cake. Place remaining green icing in a piping bag and snip off the end. Pipe large flower stems and leaves on to cake with smaller stems in-between.

★ **TO MAKE DECORATIONS,** cut sugar paste into 3 and colour with food colouring. Wrap tightly in cling film to prevent drying out.

★ Roll out sugar paste thinly, 1 piece at a time, on a surface dusted with icing sugar. Using cutters, cut out flowers and butterflies in various sizes. Leave flowers to dry on kitchen paper, and butterflies on a piece of cardboard folded and opened like a book (so they dry in the right shape) for at least 2 hrs or overnight, if you have time.

★ Arrange sugar flowers and butterflies on the cake. Dust edible lustre powders over the blossoms and butterflies for a sparkly finish, if you like.

Try this

Get creative with the decoration – drizzle over melted chocolate, and add sweets or jellies!

Giant marshmallow
CRISPY CAKE

This may be the quickest and most popular cake you've ever made!

SERVES 12 **PREP** 15 MINS, PLUS SETTING **BAKE** NONE

FOR THE CAKE

- 75g butter
- 450g mini marshmallows
- 300g rice crispy cereal
- Jelly sweets and candies to decorate, as desired

YOU WILL NEED

- A 20.5cm tin, greased and lined with non-stick baking parchment

★ Melt butter in a large pan, then gently stir in marshmallows and heat until melted, stirring constantly.

★ Add cereal and stir until well coated. Spoon half into cake tin, pressing it down really well to ensure it is flat on the base of the tin, then top with remaining mixture, pressing down firmly. You may find this easier to do with wet hands. Cover with baking parchment and press until flat. Leave to set for 3-4 hours.

★ Turn out of tin, remove paper and decorate cake with sweets of your choice. If necessary, use a little buttercream or icing sugar mixed with a little water to secure them on top of the cake.

RECIPE AND FOOD STYLING: MITZIE WILSON PROP STYLING: SUE ROWLANDS PHOTO: TOBY SCOTT

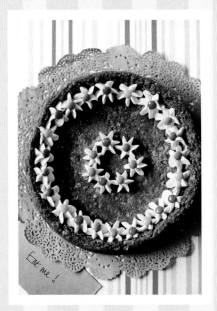

The joy of BISCUITS

An anytime treat, whether it's an afternoon pick-me-up with a cuppa or a foodie gift for a dinner party hostess

Pastel
MACARONS

Follow this foolproof method for showstopping success every time

MAKES 35 **PREP** 25 MINS **BAKE** 15 MINS

RECIPE, FOOD AND PROP STYLING: MITZIE WILSON **PHOTO:** KATIE WILSON

FOR THE MACARONS
- 120g egg whites (about 4 medium whites)
- 175g icing sugar
- 165g ground almonds
- 165g caster or granulated sugar
- Concentrated paste food colourings

FOR THE FILLING
- 300ml double cream, whipped
- 6tbsp jam

YOU WILL NEED
- 2 baking trays, lined with baking parchment
- Sugar thermometer
- 3 large piping bags and a plain 1cm nozzle

★ Preheat oven to gas mark 3/170°C (150°C in a fan oven).

★ Place half of the egg whites in a large bowl and the other half in the mixing bowl of an electric stand mixer.

★ Whizz icing sugar and almonds in a food processor until smooth, then sieve to remove any small grains. Tip mixture into egg whites in large bowl and beat until it forms a thick paste.

★ Place sugar in a small pan with 50ml water. Heat gently, then bring to the boil and stir, once or twice, with sugar thermometer to ensure sugar has dissolved (if crystals form on side of pan, wash them down with a wet pastry brush). Boil until it reaches 110°C, then whisk egg whites in stand mixer to firm peaks, keeping an eye on the syrup. As soon as it reaches 118°C, remove from the heat.

★ With mixer running, trickle syrup down the side of the bowl into egg whites until you have a smooth, shiny meringue.

★ Add meringue to almond mixture and, using a metal spoon, fold together until smooth. Divide mixture between 3 bowls. Add a little colouring to each.

★ Place 1 mixture into a piping bag fitted with a wide plain nozzle and pipe macarons on to baking tray, twisting piping bag and lifting away quickly – any points should disappear but, if not, soften them with a damp finger. They won't spread much, so can be piped fairly close to each other. Repeat process with other mixtures. Leave to rest for 3 mins (to form a smooth surface and a 'foot' when baked).

★ Bake macarons for 14 mins. Open oven after 7 mins and cover with baking parchment to prevent browning. When cooked, they will lift easily from parchment. If they stick, bake for 1-2 mins more. Leave to cool on parchment on a wire rack, then sandwich together with cream and jam.

★ Will keep for 1 day in a fridge or, unfilled, for 2-3 days in a tin.

Shortbread FINGERS

A Scottish must-have, shortbread is also excellent served with a butterscotch mousse to end a meal – and easy to bake a day ahead

MAKES 32 FINGERS **PREP** 20 MINS **BAKE** 1 HR 30 MINS

FOR THE SHORTBREAD

- 375g plain flour
- 125g caster sugar, plus extra for dusting
- 75g ground rice or fine semolina
- 300g butter

YOU WILL NEED

- A 20.5cm x 30.5cm shallow tin, lightly greased

★ Preheat oven to gas mark 2/150°C (130°C in a fan oven).

★ Add flour, sugar and ground rice to a large mixing bowl, then add butter and rub together, using your fingertips, until it looks like breadcrumbs.

★ Tip mixture into tin and spread it around evenly, then press down into edges with the back of a wooden spoon. Make fork prints all over mixture, then bake in oven for 1 hr-1 hr 30 mins or until lightly golden. Don't let it brown – or it will be overcooked.

★ Remove tin from oven and mark shortbread into fingers with a knife. Sprinkle over a little sugar, if you wish, and leave to cool, then remove from tin and serve.

RECIPE, FOOD AND PROP STYLING: HEATHER WHINNEY PHOTO: WILLIAM SHAW

Try this

For best results, don't use a fan oven for baking shortbread, as the oven will be too hot.

Vanilla cream OREOS

So much nicer than the shop-bought variety and perfect for a coffee break

MAKES ABOUT 16 **PREP** 20 MINS, PLUS CHILLING **BAKE** 15 MINS

RECIPE AND FOOD STYLING: MITZIE WILSON **PROP STYLING:** SUE ROWLANDS **PHOTO:** TOBY SCOTT

FOR THE DOUGH

- 150g butter
- 225g caster sugar
- 1 egg
- 150g plain flour, plus extra for dusting
- 75g cocoa powder

FOR THE FILLING

- 50g butter, softened
- 150g full-fat cream cheese
- 150g icing sugar
- ½tsp vanilla paste

YOU WILL NEED

- A 7.5cm round cutter
- 2 baking trays, lined with baking parchment

★ Preheat oven to gas mark 4/180°C (160°C in a fan oven).

★ **TO MAKE BISCUIT DOUGH** Using a wooden spoon or electric mixer, beat together butter and sugar until light and creamy, then beat in egg, flour and cocoa powder to make a stiff dough. Bring mixture together in a ball and wrap in cling film. Chill for 30 mins or until firm enough to roll out.

★ Lightly dust a work surface with flour and roll out half of the dough to the thickness of a £1 coin. Make sure that you move the dough around while rolling, so it doesn't stick to the surface.

★ Using a round cutter, cut out biscuits and place on baking trays, leaving a little space between each (they won't spread too much). Re-roll any trimmings and cut out more biscuits, then repeat process with remaining dough.

★ Bake for 10-12 mins, then leave to cool on trays for 10 mins. Remove with a palette knife to a wire rack to cool completely.

★ **TO MAKE FILLING,** beat butter in a bowl until really soft and smooth, then beat in cream cheese until smooth. Add icing sugar and vanilla paste and mix evenly. Sandwich biscuits together with filling and serve within a couple of hours.

Shortbread
FLOWERS

These raspberry and almond biscuits are lovely on their own, but also go well with a bowl of ice cream

MAKES 20 **PREP** 20 MINS, PLUS CHILLING **BAKE** 15 MINS

FOR THE DOUGH

- 200g plain flour, plus extra for dusting
- 225g butter, softened
- 100g icing sugar
- 100g ground almonds
- 2 drops of almond extract
- 2tsp dried raspberry pieces

YOU WILL NEED

- A flower cutter
- 2-3 baking trays, lined with baking parchment

★ Place flour and butter in a bowl and, using your fingertips, rub together until it resembles crumbs. Stir in icing sugar, ground almonds and almond extract, then add raspberry pieces and mix together until it binds to a dough. Chill if dough is a little sticky.

★ Roll out dough on a lightly floured work surface and, using a cutter, cut into flower shapes. Place biscuits on baking trays and chill for 15-20 mins.

★ Preheat oven to gas mark 4/180°C (160°C in a fan oven).

★ Remove baking trays from fridge and bake biscuits for 12-15 mins. Leave to cool on trays for 10 mins before moving to a wire rack to cool completely.

RECIPE, FOOD AND PROP STYLING: MITZIE WILSON PHOTO: KATIE WILSON

Chocolate, cherry + nut
BISCUITS

So rich and delicious, these chocolate bars are so easy to make – with no baking required!

SERVES 10 **PREP** 15 MINS, PLUS SETTING **BAKE** NONE

YOU WILL NEED

- 150g butter
- 250g plain chocolate (70% cocoa), broken into pieces
- 2tbsp golden syrup
- 50g pack sour cherries or undyed glacé cherries, roughly chopped
- 75g unskinned almonds, roughly chopped
- 50g pistachios, chopped
- 250g dried fruit (such as prunes, raisins, sultanas), roughly chopped
- 450g pack digestive biscuits, crushed
- Cocoa powder, for dusting

YOU WILL NEED

- A 30.5cm x 23cm shallow tin, lightly greased and lined

★ **TO MAKE BISCUITS,** add butter, chocolate and syrup to a pan set over a low heat and allow to melt together, stirring occasionally. Remove from the heat.

★ Add cherries, nuts, dried fruit and biscuits to chocolate mixture and stir everything together really well.

★ Spoon mixture into tin and press down on it, then leave to cool completely before putting it in the fridge to set.

★ Remove the set mixture from the tin and dust with cocoa powder. Slice into fingers to serve.

Giant celebration COOKIE CAKE

This deliciously chewy flapjack-style cookie makes a great gift decorated with a special personalised greeting

SERVES 8 **PREP** 20 MINS **BAKE** 20 MINS

FOR THE FLAPJACK
- 125g self-raising flour
- 125g porridge oats
- ½tsp bicarbonate of soda
- 125g unsalted butter
- 100g light muscovado sugar
- 3tbsp golden syrup

FOR THE ICING:
- 50g butter, at room temperature
- 150g icing sugar
- A little green food colouring
- Mini Smarties

YOU WILL NEED
- An 18cm round cake tin, greased and lined
- A medium piping bag
- A large star nozzle

★ Preheat oven to gas mark 4/180°C (160°C in a fan oven).

★ Mix together flour, oats and bicarbonate of soda in a bowl.

★ Place butter in a pan and allow to melt. Add sugar and syrup and cook for just 1 min until warmed through – do not boil. Add flour and oat mixture and stir well. Pack mixture into cake tin and press down evenly.

★ Bake for 15-18 mins. It will still feel very soft in the centre, but will firm up as it cools. Don't overcook or it will be too crisp.

★ Remove cookie cake from oven and flatten centre by placing a plate that is 2cm smaller than the cake on top of it. Press down to squash it slightly, so that a little rim forms around the edge. Allow to cool completely in the tin.

★ **TO DECORATE,** mix together butter and icing sugar until light and creamy. Add a little food colouring to desired shade, then place in a piping bag fitted with a star nozzle. Pipe flowers in the centre and around the inside rim of the cookie cake, then add Mini Smarties.

RECIPE AND FOOD STYLING: MITZIE WILSON PROP STYLING: SUE ROWLANDS PHOTO: TOBY SCOTT

Try this

Why not write a birthday message in icing and decorate with your favourite sweets?

Eat me !

Viennese BISCUITS

Buttery and sweet, these just melt in your mouth

MAKES 20 **PREP** 30 MINS **BAKE** 20 MINS

FOR THE DOUGH

- 225g butter
- 75g golden caster sugar
- 225g self-raising flour
- A drop of vanilla extract
- Icing sugar, for dusting

YOU WILL NEED

- A piping bag and 1cm nozzle
- A baking sheet, lightly greased

★ Preheat oven to gas mark 3/170°C (150°C in a fan oven).

★ Add butter and sugar to a large bowl, or the bowl of a food processor, and beat together until pale and creamy. Add flour and vanilla extract and continue to beat until combined.

★ Spoon mixture into a piping bag fitted with a 1cm nozzle. Pipe 5cm-long fingers on to a baking sheet, leaving a space between them, as the mixture will spread.

★ Bake for 15-20 mins until biscuits are cooked and golden. Leave to cool on a wire rack, then dust with icing sugar.

RECIPE, FOOD AND PROP STYLING: HEATHER WHINNEY **PHOTO:** JON WHITAKER

Chocolate chip
COOKIES

The dark chocolate makes these a grown-up treat

MAKES 16   **PREP** 15 MINS   **BAKE** 15 MINS

FOR THE COOKIES

- 125g butter
- 150g caster sugar
- 1 egg, lightly beaten
- 1tsp vanilla extract
- 150g plain flour
- 1tbsp dark cocoa, sifted
- 1tsp baking powder
- 100g bar of plain chocolate (70% cocoa solids), broken into pieces (for the chocolate chips)

YOU WILL NEED

- 2 baking trays, lined with baking parchment

★ Preheat oven to gas mark 4/180˚C (160˚C in a fan oven).

★ Add butter and sugar to the bowl of a food processor and beat until light and fluffy. Add egg and vanilla extract and beat together until combined.

★ Add flour, cocoa and baking powder and beat again until it forms a soft dough – if it is too firm, add a sprinkle of water, and if it is too sticky, add a little flour.

★ Stir through chocolate pieces, then scoop out a little of the mixture (each the size of a walnut) and roll into a ball. Use your hands to gently flatten balls on the parchment-lined trays, then press down in the centre of each cookie with the back of a fork. Repeat process with all the mixture, leaving plenty of room between each cookie.

★ Bake for 10-12 mins – the cookies should still be slightly soft (but they will harden as they cool). Remove and leave on a wire rack to cool completely.

RECIPE, FOOD AND PROP STYLING: HEATHER WHINNEY PHOTO: WILLIAM SHAW

Pistachio BISCOTTI

These biscuits taste great dipped in dessert wine

MAKES ABOUT 20   **PREP** 20 MINS   **BAKE** 30 MINS

FOR THE BISCOTTI

- 125g caster sugar
- 125g plain flour, plus extra for dusting
- 1tsp baking powder
- 125g pistachios, roughly chopped
- 2 eggs, lightly beaten
- 1tsp vanilla extract
- Icing sugar, for dusting

YOU WILL NEED

- A baking sheet, lightly greased

★ Preheat oven to gas mark 4/180˚C (160˚C in a fan oven).

★ Place sugar, flour, baking powder and pistachios into a bowl and stir. Add eggs and vanilla extract, then mix everything together using your hands (keep them well floured as you do this, as the mixture will be quite wet).

★ Divide mixture into 2, then roll each piece into a sausage shape and sit on a baking sheet (use a little more flour, if needed). Bake for 20 mins or until a pale golden colour. Remove and slice, on the diagonal, into 1cm slices.

★ Bake biscotti for a further 5-10 mins or until they are lightly golden in colour. Leave to cool, then dust with icing sugar.

White chocolate + cranberry
COOKIES

Serve these irresistible treats while still warm from the oven

MAKES 12 **PREP** 15 MINS, PLUS CHILLING **BAKE** 15 MINS

FOR THE COOKIES
- 125g unsalted butter
- 125g light muscovado sugar
- 2 eggs, lightly beaten
- 2tsp vanilla extract
- 250g wholemeal self-raising flour
- 200g bar white chocolate, roughly chopped
- 12 pecan halves
- 75g dried cranberries

YOU WILL NEED
- 2 baking trays, lined with baking parchment

★ Preheat oven to gas mark 4/180°C (160°C in a fan oven).

★ Put butter, sugar, eggs, vanilla extract, flour and half of the chocolate into a food processor. Blend together until combined and forming into a ball. Wrap in cling film and chill for 30 mins.

★ Divide mixture into 12, then roll into balls. Arrange on baking trays, spaced well apart. Flatten each one with the heel of your hand, then top each cookie with a pecan half, a few cranberries and the rest of the chocolate.

★ Bake for 15 mins until cookies are just firm. Leave on baking trays for 5 mins to firm up a little more, then serve while warm. Or leave to cool completely on a wire rack, then store in an airtight container.

RECIPE: FELICITY BARNUM-BOBB **PHOTO:** CHARLOTTE TOLHURST

Know-how

These will keep in a tin for 1 week. Use teacup, heart and letter-shaped biscuit cutters.

Iced
BISCUITS

This biscuit dough keeps its shape, so is ideal for making different designs

MAKES 18 **PREP** 25 MINS, PLUS DECORATING **BAKE** 15 MINS

FOR THE DOUGH
- 325g plain flour, plus extra for dusting
- 200g butter
- 125g caster sugar
- Zest of 1 lemon
- 2 egg yolks

TO DECORATE
- Paste food colourings of your choice
- 250g ready-to-roll icing
- 1tbsp apricot jam, warmed and sieved
- 250g royal icing sugar

YOU WILL NEED
- Assorted biscuit cutters
- Baking trays, lined with baking parchment
- Embossed rolling pin
- Piping bag and fine writing nozzle

★ Preheat oven to gas mark 4/180°C (160°C in a fan oven).

★ **TO MAKE THE DOUGH,** place flour in a bowl, add butter and rub together with your fingertips until it resembles breadcrumbs. Stir in sugar, lemon zest and egg yolks, then bring dough together with your hands to make a ball.

★ Roll out dough on a work surface lightly dusted with flour until about 5mm thick. Cut out shapes with biscuit cutters and place on baking trays.

★ Bake for 8-12 mins, depending on size – they're ready when they are turning golden brown around the edges. Leave on baking tray for 5 mins, then allow to cool on a wire rack.

★ **TO DECORATE,** colour ready-to-roll icing as desired, then roll out thinly with embossed rolling pin (to create a pattern), if you like. Use same cutters to cut out icing shapes. Brush a thin layer of jam over biscuits and place icing on top.

★ Mix royal icing as directed on the pack and place in a piping bag with a fine writing nozzle. Pipe decorations on the biscuits.

★ **TO MAKE ICING ROSES,** tightly roll up thin strips of icing about 5mm wide to make rosebuds and arrange on biscuits, using a little icing to secure them.

RECIPE, FOOD AND PROP STYLING: MITZIE WILSON **PHOTO:** CLARE WINFIELD

Raspberry CREAMS

With their vibrant berry filling, these will stand out in any biscuit selection

MAKES 16 **PREP** 20 MINS, PLUS CHILLING **BAKE** 10 MINS

FOR THE DOUGH
- 75g butter, softened
- 125g icing sugar
- 1 medium egg, beaten
- ½tsp vanilla extract
- 200g plain flour
- 1tsp baking powder

FOR THE FILLING
- 125g raspberries
- 1tsp sugar
- 5tbsp double cream, whipped
- 150g white chocolate, melted and cooled

YOU WILL NEED
- A 4cm cookie cutter
- A baking sheet, lined with baking parchment

★ Preheat oven to gas mark 4, 180°C (160°C in a fan oven).

★ **TO MAKE DOUGH,** cream together butter and sugar until pale and fluffy. Beat in egg and vanilla, then mix in flour, baking powder and a pinch of salt until smooth. Roll out mixture between 2 pieces of cling film until the thickness of a £1 coin. Chill dough for 1 hr.

★ Cut dough into rounds with a cookie cutter and place on a baking sheet, spaced well apart. Bake for 6 to 8 mins or until a very pale golden colour. Leave to cool on baking sheet for 5 mins, then transfer to a wire rack to cool completely.

★ **FOR THE FILLING,** blend together raspberries and sugar in a food processor, then sieve to remove seeds. Stir cream and raspberry juice into white chocolate and chill for 1 hr. Sandwich cooled biscuits together with raspberry filling.

RECIPE, FOOD AND PROP STYLING: HEATHER WHINNEY **PHOTO:** IAIN BAGWELL

Try this

Line the sides and base of the tin, so it is easy to turn out and slice into bars.

Chocolate + almond
CHEWY BARS

Chocolate shortbread, topped with almonds and pistachios and drizzled with chocolate – this is the ultimate tray bake!

MAKES 24   **PREP** 25 MINS   **BAKE** 30 MINS

FOR THE BASE
- 225g plain flour
- 25g cocoa powder
- 75g caster sugar
- ½tsp baking powder
- 100g butter, cut into pieces
- 2 eggs

FOR THE TOPPING
- 150g butter
- 75g granulated sugar
- 75g light muscovado sugar
- 3tbsp golden syrup
- 4tbsp double cream
- 200g blanched almonds, cut in half
- 100g pistachios, halved
- 100g pecans, shelled
- 75g plain chocolate, chopped

YOU WILL NEED
- 30cm x 23cm tray bake tin, base and sides lined with baking parchment

★ Preheat oven to gas mark 4/180˚C (160˚C in a fan oven).

★ **TO MAKE THE BASE,** place flour, cocoa, sugar and baking powder into a mixing bowl. Add butter and rub in until mixture resembles breadcrumbs. This can be done in a food processor, if you like. Add eggs and mix to a soft dough. Press dough into the tin and spread it flat. Chill while making the topping.

★ **FOR THE TOPPING,** melt butter in a small pan, then stir in the sugars and syrup. Stir until dissolved, then bring to the boil. Add cream and boil for 1 min, stirring continuously. Remove from the heat and stir in all of the nuts.

★ Spread nut mixture evenly over the dough base, then bake for 25-30 mins until the mixture is gently bubbling. Remove from the oven, then scatter chocolate over the top (the residual heat will melt it). Leave in the tin until completely cold and set, then turn out and cut into fingers.

RECIPE, FOOD AND PROP STYLING: MITZIE WILSON PHOTO: TOBY SCOTT

Lavender + borage
GARLANDS

We used borage, lavender and tiny thyme flowers to decorate these pretty biscuits, but you can use any edible flowers, or sprinkles, if you prefer

MAKES ABOUT 20 **PREP** 20 MINS, PLUS CHILLING **BAKE** 15 MINS

FOR THE DOUGH
- 175g plain flour, plus extra for dusting
- 100g butter, chilled
- 65g golden caster sugar
- 1tsp vanilla extract
- 1 egg yolk

FOR THE ICING
- 150g icing sugar
- 1tsp lemon juice
- Borage, lavender and thyme flowers

YOU WILL NEED
- A 7cm fluted biscuit cutter
- A 3cm plain round biscuit cutter
- A baking tray, lined with baking parchment

★ Preheat oven to gas mark 4/180°C (160°C in a fan oven).

★ **TO MAKE THE DOUGH,** place flour, butter and sugar in a food processor and blend until it looks like breadcrumbs (or rub together with your fingertips).

★ Add vanilla and egg yolk and continue to mix until mixture comes together into a firm dough.

★ Turn out on to a lightly floured work surface and knead dough lightly into a ball. Wrap in cling film and chill for 30 mins, if the dough is sticky.

★ Dust a worktop lightly with flour, then roll out the dough to the thickness of a £1 coin. Using the larger round cutter, cut out your biscuits, then use the smaller cutter to cut out the centres. Place biscuits on baking tray, leaving a little space between each. Re-roll any trimmings and repeat process.

★ Bake for 10-12 mins or until a pale golden colour. Allow to cool for 10 mins on the baking trays, then leave to cool completely on a wire rack.

★ **TO MAKE THE ICING,** mix icing sugar with enough lemon juice to make a pouring consistency that will just coat the back of a spoon. Dip one side of the biscuits into the icing, then place on a wire rack to set. (If you want to keep the biscuits for a few days you can dry out the icing in an oven at 50°C fan for 30 mins.) Decorate with flowers while icing is still wet.

RECIPE, FOOD AND PROP STYLING: MITZIE WILSON PHOTO: DAN JONES

Cranberry, apricot + coconut SQUARES

These are delicious and handy for when unexpected guests drop in

MAKES 12 **PREP** 25 MINS, PLUS FIRMING **BAKE** 40 MINS

RECIPE, FOOD AND PROP STYLING: MITZIE WILSON **PHOTO:** DAN JONES

FOR THE SQUARES

- 200g plain chocolate, broken into pieces
- 100g butter, softened
- 200g caster sugar
- 100g dried apricots
- 100g dried cranberries
- 200g desiccated coconut
- Zest of 1 lime
- 2 eggs

YOU WILL NEED

- A 18cm x 28cm tray bake tin, lined with baking parchment

★ **TO MAKE THE SQUARES,** place chocolate in a bowl over a pan of gently simmering water and stir until melted, or melt in the microwave in 1-min bursts. Add chocolate to tray bake tin and spread out evenly, then put in the freezer while you make the cake mixture.

★ Heat oven to gas mark 4/180°C (160°C in a fan oven). Place butter and sugar in a mixing bowl and beat until light and fluffy.

★ Snip apricots into small pieces and add to a bowl with cranberries, coconut and lime zest. Beat eggs together and stir in until evenly mixed. Spread mixture over set chocolate in tin and level the top.

★ Bake for 40 mins, covering the top with baking parchment after 25 mins.

★ Allow to cool in tin, then refrigerate for at least 1 hr until firm. Cut in slices to serve.

★ This will keep for 1 week in a cake tin.

Gingerbread PEOPLE

Buttery, spicy and oh-so crisp, these are always winners... with children and grown-ups alike!

MAKES ABOUT 10   **PREP** 15 MINS, PLUS CHILLING   **BAKE** 15 MINS

FOR THE GINGERBREAD
- 100g butter
- 6tbsp golden syrup
- 50g light muscovado sugar
- 250g plain flour, plus extra for dusting
- ¾tsp bicarbonate of soda
- 1tbsp ground ginger

YOU WILL NEED
- A gingerbread man cutter
- 2 baking trays, lined with baking parchment

★ Preheat oven to gas mark 5/190°C (170°C in a fan oven).

★ Place butter in a pan and heat until melted. Stir in syrup and sugar and boil for 1 min. Remove from heat and leave to cool for 2-3 mins.

★ Place remaining ingredients into a mixing bowl, then gradually pour in melted butter mixture, beating well with a wooden spoon until it forms a soft dough.

★ Turn out dough on to cling film and pat out into a thick circle. Wrap and chill in fridge for about 1 hr until firm.

★ Dust a work surface with flour, then roll out dough to about the thickness of a £1 coin. Using the cutter, cut out gingerbread men and place on baking trays, spaced well apart. Bake for 12-13 mins until golden brown. Allow to cool on trays.

★ These can be stored for up to 1 week in a cake tin.

RECIPE AND FOOD STYLING: MITZIE WILSON   PROP STYLING: SUE ROWLANDS   PHOTO: TOBY SCOTT

Feathered shortbread
HEARTS

*These deliciously buttery biscuits can be cut
into any shape you like*

MAKES 16 **PREP** 25 MINS, PLUS DRYING **BAKE** 15 MINS

FOR THE SHORTBREAD

- 100g butter, at room temperature
- 50g icing sugar
- Zest of ½ lemon
- 75g cornflour
- ½tsp baking powder
- 75g plain flour, plus extra for dusting

FOR THE ICING

- 250g royal icing sugar
- Concentrated food colourings, as desired

YOU WILL NEED

- A 7cm heart-shaped biscuit cutter
- 2 baking trays, lined with baking parchment
- 2 plastic piping bags
- Cocktail stick or skewer

★ Preheat oven to gas mark 4/180°C (160°C in a fan oven).

★ Place butter and icing sugar in a mixing bowl and beat together with a wooden spoon until smooth. Beat in lemon zest, cornflour, baking powder and flour until mixture comes together in a firm dough. Gather together with your hands then wrap in cling film and chill for 15-20 mins, if necessary.

★ Roll out dough on a lightly floured surface until the thickness of a £1 coin. Use a heart cutter to stamp out the biscuits, re-rolling dough as necessary.

★ Place biscuits on baking trays and bake for around 12 mins until just golden around the edges. Allow to cool completely.

★ **FOR THE ICING**, mix icing sugar with water, as directed on the pack. Divide between 2 bowls and add food colourings, then keep it covered with cling film. Using 2 piping bags, place half of each icing in a bag. Snip off the ends of the bags when ready to use. Mix remaining icing with enough water to make a thick pouring consistency.

★ **TO DECORATE**, work on 4 biscuits at a time. First pipe an outline around the edge of the biscuits. Then spoon a little of the runnier icing inside, easing the icing to the edges with a cocktail stick. Using a piping bag, pipe contrasting lines of icing across the biscuits. Drag a cocktail stick first in one direction then in the other direction to create a feathered effect. Leave to dry for a couple of hours (or bake for 30 mins at 50°C)

RECIPE, FOOD AND PROP STYLING: MITZIE WILSON **PHOTO:** TOBY SCOTT

English
MACAROONS

Crisp on the outside and chewy inside, these are perfect served with a cuppa

MAKES 25 **PREP** 15 MINS **BAKE** 25 MINS

FOR THE BISCUITS

- 2 large egg whites
- 100g ground almonds
- 175g caster sugar
- 25g ground rice or semolina
- A few drops of almond extract
- About 25 whole blanched almonds

YOU WILL NEED

- 2 baking trays, lined with baking parchment

★ Preheat oven to gas mark 2/150°C (130°C in a fan oven).

★ Place egg whites in a clean, grease-free bowl and whisk until soft peaks form. Stir in ground almonds, sugar, ground rice or semolina and almond extract.

★ Roll mixture into large marble-sized balls with damp hands, as mixture is quite sticky. Place on baking trays, allowing room for macaroons to spread about 3 times their size. Place a whole almond in the centre of each and bake for 20-25 mins until a pale golden brown. Leave to cool on baking trays, then serve.

★ The biscuits can be stored for up to 1 week in a cake tin.

RECIPE AND FOOD STYLING: MITZIE WILSON PROP STYLING: SUE ROWLANDS PHOTO: TOBY SCOTT

Choc-dipped shortbread
SQUARES

Dark chocolate makes these doubly delicious

MAKES 9 **PREP** 15 MINS, PLUS SETTING **BAKE** 40 MINS

RECIPE, FOOD AND PROP STYLING: MITZIE WILSON PHOTO: TOBY SCOTT

FOR THE BISCUITS
- 100g plain flour, plus extra for dusting
- 50g semolina
- 100g softened butter
- 50g caster sugar
- 50g plain chocolate chips

TO DECORATE
- 100g plain chocolate

YOU WILL NEED
- A baking tray, lined with baking parchment

★ Preheat oven to gas mark 2/150°C (130°C in a fan oven).

★ **TO MAKE BISCUITS,** place flour and semolina in food processor with the butter and process until mixture resembles breadcrumbs (or rub together with your fingers). Stir in the sugar and chocolate chips. Squeeze the mixture together to make a firm dough.

★ Roll out dough on a lightly floured work surface into a 20cm square. Cut into squares and place biscuits on to a baking tray, allowing a little space between them.

★ Bake for 40 mins or until the biscuits are a pale golden colour. Allow the shortbread to cool on the baking tray.

★ **TO DECORATE,** melt chocolate in a microwave for 1 min or in a bowl over gently simmering water. Dip base of biscuits in chocolate and place on baking parchment. Chill until set.

★ These will keep for up to 1 week in a cake tin.

Honey + oat flapjack
COOKIES

*These have a lovely chewy texture
and are so moreish*

MAKES 40   **PREP** 10 MINS, PLUS CHILLING   **BAKE** 10 MINS

FOR THE COOKIES

- 150g butter
- 150g soft light brown sugar
- 75g blossom honey
- 75g plain flour
- 1tsp ground nutmeg
- ½tsp bicarbonate of soda
- 200g jumbo rolled oats
- 1 medium egg, beaten

YOU WILL NEED

- A baking sheet, lined with baking parchment

★ Preheat oven to gas mark 2, 150°C (130°C in a fan oven).

★ In a small pan set over a medium heat, melt together butter, sugar and honey. Once butter has melted, stir in the rest of the ingredients, then chill in the fridge for 1 hr or until set.

★ Roll mixture into walnut-sized pieces, place on a baking sheet and flatten gently with your hand. Bake for 8 to 10 mins until golden. Leave to cool.

RECIPE AND FOOD STYLING: KATY GREENWOOD   PROP STYLING: HEATHER WHINNEY   PHOTO: IAIN BAGWELL

The joy of
CHRISTMAS

Get your festive baking sorted with these delicious ideas
– perfect for sharing with friends and family

Chelsea bun Christmas TREE

This makes a great centrepiece for your festive table and everyone can tear and share the buns!

MAKES 16 BUNS **PREP** 30 MINS, PLUS PROVING **BAKE** 30 MINS

RECIPE AND FOOD STYLING: MITZIE WILSON **PROP STYLING:** SUE ROWLANDS **PHOTO:** TOBY SCOTT

FOR THE BUNS

- 500g strong white bread flour, plus extra for dusting
- 1tsp salt
- 15g butter
- 7g sachet of easy bake yeast
- 250ml milk
- 2 eggs
- 25g butter, melted
- Few sugar cubes, crushed (optional)

FOR THE FILLING

- 50g golden caster sugar
- 2tsp ground cinnamon
- 75g raisins
- 75g dried cranberries
- 50g chopped mixed peel

YOU WILL NEED

- A large baking tray, lined with baking parchment

★ **TO MAKE BUNS,** place flour, salt and butter in a large mixing bowl. Rub in butter until it makes crumbs, then stir in yeast. Warm milk until it's just hand-hot, then add to flour mixture with eggs. Beat well until it comes to a soft dough. Turn out on a lightly floured work surface and knead for 10 mins by hand.

★ Roll out dough to a rectangle about 30.5cm x 25.5cm.

★ **FOR THE FILLING,** sprinkle caster sugar, cinnamon, dried fruit and mixed peel over dough, then roll up like a Swiss roll.

★ Cut into slices about 15cm x 3cm thick and arrange on a baking tray in a Christmas-tree shape. Cover with oiled cling film and leave in a warm place until doubled in size.

★ Preheat oven to gas mark 5/190°C (170°C in a fan oven). Brush buns with butter and bake for 30 mins until golden brown. Sprinkle with crushed sugar cubes, if you like.

Chocolate BOMBE

Try a new take on the traditional Christmas pudding with this chocolate-covered spiced fruit cake

SERVES 12 **PREP** 30 MINS, PLUS COOLING **BAKE** 1 HR 20 MINS

FOR THE FRUIT CAKE

- 200g butter, softened
- 225g light muscovado sugar
- 4 eggs
- 200g plain flour
- 50g cocoa powder, sifted
- 150g plain chocolate drops
- 200g dried sour cherries
- 100g dried cranberries
- 250g sultanas
- 200g raisins
- ½tsp ground cinnamon
- ½tsp mixed spice

TO DECORATE

- 3tbsp apricot jam, warmed and sieved
- 500g chocolate-flavoured sugar paste
- A little icing sugar, for dusting
- 100g white chocolate
- 50g plain chocolate
- 4 fresh holly leaves
- 3 glacé cherries

YOU WILL NEED

- 2 x 16cm hemisphere cake tins (try Lakeland)
- A small paintbrush

★ Preheat oven to gas mark 3/170°C (150°C in a fan oven).

★ Beat butter and sugar together in a bowl until creamy. Gradually beat in eggs. Stir in the rest of the cake ingredients and spoon into cake tins.

★ Bake for 20 mins, then reduce oven temperature to gas mark 2/150°C (130°C in a fan oven) and bake for 1 hr more until a skewer comes out clean when inserted in the centre. Allow to cool in the tin for 1 hr, then turn out and leave to cool completely.

★ **TO DECORATE**, spread a little jam over the top of 1 cake. Sandwich cakes together and spread jam all over.

★ Roll out sugar paste on a worktop dusted with icing sugar until large enough to cover cake – with an extra 5cm-6cm. Drape over cake, easing out the pleats, then cut off any excess.

★ Melt white chocolate in a bowl over gently simmering water, then pour over cake and leave to set.

★ Melt plain chocolate in the same way and brush over the back of the holly leaves with a small paintbrush. Leave to set, then carefully peel away and discard fresh leaves. Decorate cake with chocolate holly leaves and cherries.

★ The bombe will keep for 4-5 days in a cake tin.

RECIPE AND FOOD STYLING: MITZIE WILSON **PROP STYLING:** SUE ROWLANDS **PHOTO:** TOBY SCOTT

Try this

If you only have 1 hemisphere cake mould, just bake half the cake at a time.

Try this
Omit the ginger, if you prefer, and decorate with chocolate curls or candied fruit.

Chocolate, ginger + cherry GARLAND

This looks splendid and tastes fabulous – and makes a perfect alternative to a traditional Christmas cake

SERVES 12   PREP 45 MINS   BAKE 50 MINS

RECIPE AND FOOD STYLING: MITZIE WILSON **PROP STYLING:** SUE ROWLANDS **PHOTO:** CLARE WINFIELD

FOR THE CAKE

- 200g butter, softened
- 200g caster sugar
- 4 eggs, beaten
- 200g self-raising flour
- 50g ground almonds
- 25g cocoa powder
- 100g glacé cherries, halved
- 75g dried cranberries
- 50g crystallised ginger, chopped
- 100g plain chocolate chips

TO DECORATE

- 75g plain chocolate
- Glacé cherries
- Edible gold leaf
- A few pieces crystallised ginger, roughly sliced
- Red sugar balls
- Bronze sugar sprinkles

YOU WILL NEED

- A 1.5 litre ring mould, greased

★ Preheat oven to gas mark 5, 190°C (170°C in a fan oven).

★ **TO MAKE CAKE,** cream together butter and sugar in a bowl until really light and fluffy. Gradually beat in eggs until smooth, adding a little flour if the mixture starts to curdle.

★ Add ground almonds, cocoa powder and the rest of the flour to the bowl. Then add cherries, cranberries, crystallised ginger and chocolate chips and mix together well.

★ Add mixture to ring mould and spread out evenly, then bake for 45-50 mins or until firm to the touch. Turn cake upside down on a wire rack and leave to cool for 10 mins before removing from the tin. Leave to cool completely.

★ **TO DECORATE,** melt chocolate in a bowl over a pan of gently simmering water, then drizzle over the top of the cake.

★ Roll glacé cherries in gold leaf and arrange on top of the cake with the crystallised ginger, sugar balls and sugar sprinkles.

Reindeer cake CUBES

Decorated with cute reindeers, these individual Christmas cake squares are perfect with a cup of tea. Yum!

CUTS INTO 16 SQUARES PREP 20 MINS BAKE 50 MINS

FOR THE FRUIT CAKE

- 125g butter, softened
- 125g dark muscovado sugar
- 3 eggs, beaten
- 150g plain flour
- 250g raisins
- 100g sultanas
- 100g dried cranberries
- 50g mixed candied peel
- 1tsp ground cinnamon
- ½tsp mixed spice
- Zest of 1 orange and juice of ½

TO DECORATE

- 1tbsp apricot jam, warmed and sieved
- A little icing sugar, for dusting
- 300g marzipan
- 250g sugar paste
- A little brown food colouring
- A little white lustre powder (optional)

YOU WILL NEED

- A 18cm x 28cm tray bake tin, lined with baking parchment
- A small reindeer cutter

★ Preheat oven to gas mark 4, 180°C (160°C in a fan oven).

★ **FOR THE FRUIT CAKE,** beat together butter and sugar until light and fluffy. Gradually add eggs, beating until smooth, then fold in flour, dried fruit, candied peel, spices and orange zest and juice. Add to tray bake tin and spread out evenly.

★ Bake for 45-50 mins until firm and springy in the centre. Allow to cool in the tin for 10 mins, then turn out and allow to cool completely upside down on a wire rack.

★ Spread the bottom of the cake (this will now be the top) with jam. Dust a work surface with icing sugar and roll out marzipan to a rectangle the same size as the cake, then lay on top, trimming the edges.

★ Colour 50g of the sugar paste with food colouring and roll out on a work surface dusted with icing sugar. Using a cutter, cut out 16 reindeers and set aside on baking parchment. Dust with a little lustre powder, if you like.

★ Roll out the remaining sugar paste in the same way as the marzipan. Brush marzipan with a little boiled water and lay sugar paste on top of it. Trim to fit, then cut cake into squares and decorate with reindeers.

★ The cakes will keep for up to 1 week in a cake tin.

RECIPE AND FOOD STYLING: MITZIE WILSON PROP STYLING: SUE ROWLANDS PHOTO: TOBY SCOTT

Gift parcel CAKES

One square cake will make four individual icing-wrapped 'parcels', which can be given as delicious gifts

MAKES 4 CAKES **PREP** 30 MINS, PLUS DECORATING **BAKE** 1 HR

RECIPE AND FOOD STYLING: MITZIE WILSON **PROP STYLING:** SUE ROWLANDS **PHOTO:** CLARE WINFIELD

FOR THE CAKE
- 225g butter, softened
- 300g caster sugar
- 5 eggs, beaten
- 350g plain flour
- 2tsp baking powder
- 1tsp mixed spice
- Zest of 1 orange
- 4tbsp orange juice
- 100g mixed dried fruit or raisins
- 75g dried cranberries

TO DECORATE
- 4tbsp apricot jam, warmed and sieved
- Icing sugar, for dusting
- 750g almond paste
- 750g sugar paste
- Red and green food colouring paste

YOU WILL NEED
- A 20cm square cake tin, lined with baking parchment
- 4 x 10cm square cake cards
- Cookie/icing cutters
- Red and green ribbon

★ Preheat oven to gas mark 4, 180°C (160°C in a fan oven).

★ **TO MAKE THE CAKE,** cream butter and sugar together until really light and fluffy, then gradually beat in eggs until smooth, adding a little flour if the mixture begins to curdle.

★ Fold in the rest of the flour, and the baking powder, mixed spice, orange zest and juice and all the dried fruit. Mix well.

★ Add mixture to the cake tin, spread out evenly and bake for 50 mins-1 hr or until golden brown and firm (when a skewer is inserted in the centre, it should come out clean – if not, return to the oven for a few more minutes). Allow to cool in the tin for 10 mins, then remove from the tin and leave to cool on a wire rack.

★ **TO DECORATE,** cut cake into 4 equal squares. Spread apricot jam over each and place on a cake card.

★ Dust a worktop with icing sugar. Divide almond paste into 4 and roll out 1 portion into a square that's large enough to cover the top and sides of 1 square cake. Smooth almond paste on to cake, lifting the skirt of the paste to ease out pleats at the corners, then trim. Repeat process with the remaining cakes.

★ Brush each cake very lightly with boiled water, then roll out the sugar paste and cover the cakes in the same way.

★ Colour the icing trimmings with a little red or green food colouring, then roll out thinly. Stamp out decorations with the cutters, then press on to the cakes and decorate with ribbons.

★ These cakes will keep for 5-6 days in a cake tin.

Christmas tree
CAKE

A Yuletide showstopper that you can make ahead of the festive rush

SERVES 16 **PREP** 30 MINS **BAKE** 4 HRS

FOR THE FRUIT CAKE
- 800g mixed dried fruit
- 250g plain flour
- 50g chopped mixed nuts
- 2tsp mixed spice
- 1tsp ground cinnamon
- 1tsp vanilla or almond essence
- Zest of 1 lemon and 1 orange
- 225g butter
- 225g light muscovado sugar
- 5 eggs, beaten

TO DECORATE
- 3tbsp apricot jam, warmed and sieved
- 700g almond paste
- A little icing sugar, for dusting
- 1kg white sugar paste
- Green and red paste food colouring
- A few sugar cubes, crushed
- Edible silver balls

YOU WILL NEED
- A 23cm round cake tin, greased and double lined with baking parchment
- A 25.5cm round drum cake board
- Star plunger cutters (available from Hobbycraft)

★ Preheat oven to gas mark 2/150°C (130°C in a fan oven).

★ **FOR THE FRUIT CAKE,** place dried fruit, flour (reserve 1-2tbsp), nuts, spices, vanilla and lemon and orange zests in a large mixing bowl.

★ In another large bowl, beat together butter and sugar until light, creamy and pale in colour. Gradually whisk in eggs, beating well after each addition. Add a little of the reserved flour, if necessary, to prevent curdling. Add fruit mixture, stir, then add to the baking tin and smooth the top.

★ Bake in the centre of the oven for 30 mins, then reduce oven temperature to gas mark 1/140°C (120°C in a fan oven) and cook for 3 hrs-3 hrs 30 mins more until it's firm to the touch and a dark golden colour. Leave to cool completely in the tin, then turn out.

★ **TO DECORATE,** brush jam all over cake. Roll out almond paste on a work surface, lightly dusted with icing sugar, until

large enough to cover top and sides of cake. Drape over cake and trim edge.

★ Roll out 650g of the sugar paste in the same way, making it a little larger than the cake, and drape over the top and sides of cake. Trim the excess and wrap in cling film.

★ Using trimmings, colour around 300g of the sugar paste pale green. Roll out half thinly in a circle to cover a dampened cake board. Colour 150g of the sugar paste red. Wrap all icings in cling film when not using. Roll out a 15cm circle of green icing and place in the centre of the cake. Roll out white icing, cut out stars in various sizes and form into a tree shape on green circle on cake.

★ Roll remaining green, white and red icings into long thin sausage shapes, twist together and wrap around green circle on the top and base of the cake. Sprinkle over sugar and decorate with silver balls. Place board on plate to serve.

RECIPE AND FOOD STYLING: MITZIE WILSON **PROP STYLING:** SUE ROWLANDS **PHOTO:** TOBY SCOTT

Try this

Make this fruit cake a month in advance, if you have the time, so it can mature before you ice it.

Cranberry ROULADE

The cranberries add a delicious sharpness to the sweet meringue and look very festive, too!

SERVES 8-10 **PREP** 30 MINS **BAKE** 25 MINS

RECIPE AND FOOD STYLING: MITZIE WILSON **PROP STYLING:** SUE ROWLANDS **PHOTO:** CLARE WINFIELD

FOR THE MERINGUE

- **4 egg whites**
- **200g caster sugar**

FOR THE FILLING

- **100g cranberries**
- **Zest and juice of ½ an orange**
- **75g-100g caster sugar**
- **300ml double cream**

YOU WILL NEED

- **33cm x 23cm Swiss roll tin, lined with baking parchment**

★ Preheat oven to gas mark 3, 170°C (150°C in a fan oven).

★ **TO MAKE MERINGUE,** place egg whites in a clean, grease-free bowl and whisk until they form stiff peaks. Add the sugar, 1tbsp at a time, whisking until mixture is glossy and stands in stiff peaks.

★ Spread meringue evenly in the tin and bake for 25 mins until turning a pale golden colour. Leave in the tin until completely cool, then turn out on to a sheet of baking parchment.

★ **FOR THE FILLING,** heat cranberries, orange zest and juice and 75g of the caster sugar in a pan for 10 mins or until cranberries are soft. Add more sugar, if you like. Tip into a bowl and leave to cool. Reserve a few whole cooked cranberries for decoration, then strain sauce through a sieve into a bowl, reserving the juices – the sauce shouldn't be too runny or it will ooze through the meringue.

★ When ready to serve, whip cream until it just holds its shape. Spread a thin layer of cranberry sauce over the meringue, top with cream, then roll up from the short end, using the baking parchment to help you. Place on a plate, decorate with reserved cranberries and a drizzle of sauce (serve the rest on the side).

★ Keep in the fridge and serve within 1 hr.

Fondant
FANCIES

These lovely light sponges look so pretty and, by using different cutters, can be tailor-made for any occasion

---

MAKES 25 **PREP** 1 HR 30 MINS, PLUS CHILLING **BAKE** 45 MINS

FOR THE SPONGE
- 250g butter, softened
- 250g caster sugar
- 5 eggs, beaten
- 250g self-raising flour
- 1tsp vanilla extract

FOR THE ICING
- 125g butter, softened
- 200g icing sugar, plus extra for dusting
- 3tbsp apricot jam
- 250g marzipan
- 750g fondant icing sugar
- 100g green sugar paste
- White sugar ball sprinkles

YOU WILL NEED
- 20cm square cake tin, greased and lined with baking parchment
- Festive shape cutters

★ Preheat oven to gas mark 4/180˚C (160˚C in a fan oven).

★ **TO MAKE THE SPONGE,** place butter and sugar in a mixing bowl and beat until really light and creamy. Gradually beat in the eggs, a little at a time, then stir in half of the flour and the vanilla extract. Fold in the remaining flour and add mixture to cake tin.

★ Bake for 35-45 mins until golden brown and firm to the touch. To test, insert a skewer into the centre; it should come out clean – if not, return to the oven for a few more minutes. Allow to cool in the tin for 10 mins, then turn out upside down on to a wire rack and leave to cool completely.

★ **FOR THE ICING,** mix together the butter, icing sugar and a drop of boiling water until smooth.

★ When the sponge is cold, spread the top (ie the flat base of the cake) with apricot jam.

★ Dust a worktop with icing sugar and roll out the marzipan very thinly. Place on top of the cake, trimming it to fit.

★ Cut cake into 5 x 4cm strips, then cut each strip into 5 x 4cm squares (so you have 25 cakes). Spread the 4 sides – but not the top of each little cake – very thinly with icing. Chill cakes for 30 mins in the fridge.

★ Mix fondant icing sugar with just enough water to give a very thick pouring consistency – it should thickly coat the back of a spoon. To ice cakes, pour a little fondant icing over each one and, with a small palette knife, spread icing down the sides. Leave to set on a wire rack or board. Roll out green sugar paste thinly, stamp out shapes with the cutters and press on top of each cake, along with the sugar ball sprinkles.

RECIPE AND FOOD STYLING: MITZIE WILSON PROP STYLING: SUE ROWLANDS PHOTO: CLARE WINFIELD

Try this

If the biscuits become a little soft before you hang them, dry out in a low oven for 5 mins.

Gingerbread heart advent
CALENDAR

*Make a gingerbread heart for every day of the month
and hang them as decorations for a Christmas party*

MAKES 24 **PREP** 45 MINS, PLUS FIRMING **BAKE** 15 MINS

RECIPE AND FOOD STYLING: MITZIE WILSON PROP STYLING: SUE ROWLANDS PHOTOS: CLARE WINFIELD

FOR THE BISCUIT DOUGH
- 350g plain flour, plus extra for dusting
- 1tsp bicarbonate of soda
- 2tbsp ground ginger
- 1tbsp ground cinnamon
- 150g chilled butter, cut into chunks
- 175g light muscovado sugar
- 2tbsp golden syrup
- 1 egg

TO DECORATE
- 250g royal icing sugar
- Concentrated red food colouring

YOU WILL NEED
- A 10cm heart biscuit cutter
- 2 or 3 baking trays, lined with baking parchment
- A paintbrush
- Piping bags and fine writing nozzle
- Thin red ribbon

★ Preheat oven to gas mark 4/180°C (160°C in a fan oven).

★ **TO MAKE DOUGH,** mix together flour, bicarbonate of soda, ground ginger and cinnamon. Add butter, then rub in with your fingertips until mixture resembles breadcrumbs.

★ Stir in sugar, syrup and egg. Using your hands, gather mixture together in a bowl and knead lightly until smooth. Place in the fridge (or even the freezer) to firm up.

★ Dust a worktop with flour and roll out biscuit dough to the thickness of a £1 coin. Using the cutter, stamp out 24 hearts, re-rolling the dough as necessary. Place hearts on baking trays and, using the end of a small paintbrush, make a hole near the top of each heart where you will thread the ribbon.

★ Bake biscuits for 10-12 mins or until turning golden brown at the edges. Remove from the oven and pierce each one again with the paintbrush to make sure the holes have not closed up. Allow to cool for 10 mins on the baking tray, then leave to cool completely on a wire rack.

★ **TO DECORATE,** make up royal icing as directed on the pack and colour three-quarters of it to the desired red shade, leaving the rest white. Place red icing in a piping bag with a fine nozzle and pipe a pattern around the edge of each biscuit. Use the white icing for the numbers. Thread red ribbon through the small holes so you can hang up the biscuits.

★ These biscuits will keep for up to 1 month in a cake tin.

Gold holly CUPCAKES

We made orange cupcakes topped with holly leaves, but you can use almond, chocolate or lemon cakes, if you prefer

MAKES 12 PREP 50 MINS BAKE 25 MINS

FOR THE CUPCAKES

- 150g butter, at room temperature
- 150g golden caster sugar
- 3 eggs, beaten
- 150g self-raising flour
- Zest of 1 orange
- 1tbsp orange juice
- 100g white ready-to-roll sugar paste

FOR THE ICING

- 150g butter, softened
- 300g icing sugar, plus extra for dusting
- ½tsp vanilla extract

YOU WILL NEED

- A 12-hole cupcake tin, lined with paper cases
- A piping bag
- A large star nozzle
- A holly cutter
- Edible gold and red lustre powders

★ Preheat oven to gas mark 4/180°C (160°C in a fan oven).

★ **TO MAKE CUPCAKES,** add butter and caster sugar to a mixing bowl and beat with a wooden spoon or electric whisk until light and fluffy.

★ Add eggs, a little at a time, beating well after each addition. Add 1-2tbsp flour to prevent mixture curdling. Mix in orange zest and juice, then fold in the remaining flour with a large metal spoon.

★ Divide mixture equally between cupcake cases and bake for 20-25 mins until golden brown and just firm to the touch. Allow to cool for 10 mins in the tin, then remove and leave to cool completely on a wire rack.

★ **TO MAKE ICING,** beat together butter, icing sugar and vanilla until smooth and creamy, adding a drop of boiling water, if necessary. Place in a piping bag fitted with a star nozzle and pipe swirls on to each cake.

★ Roll out sugar paste thinly on a worktop dusted with icing sugar and cut out 36 leaves with the holly cutter. Shape them so they are slightly curved, then leave to dry on kitchen paper. Roll trimmings into 36 small balls (to use as berries).

★ Place a drop of water on a saucer, add a little gold lustre powder and mix to a paste, then brush over holly leaves with a fine brush. Arrange 3 on each cake. Roll small balls in red lustre powder and arrange 'berries' in the centre of the leaves.

★ Undecorated cakes will keep for 3 days in a cake tin.

RECIPE, FOOD AND PROP STYLING: MITZIE WILSON PHOTO: HEARST STUDIOS

Try this

Instead of chocolate, mix icing sugar with enough water to make a pouring consistency, then spread over biscuits.

Chocolate–decorated
LEBKUCHEN

These German spiced biscuits are soft and chewy. Leave them plain or decorate with melted chocolate or a glacé icing

MAKES ABOUT 12 **PREP** 30 MINS, PLUS CHILLING **BAKE** 15 MINS

RECIPE AND FOOD STYLING: MITZIE WILSON PROP STYLING: SUE ROWLANDS PHOTO: TOBY SCOTT

FOR THE BISCUITS
- 250g plain flour, plus extra for dusting
- 75g ground almonds
- 2tsp ground ginger
- 1tsp ground cinnamon
- Pinch of ground cloves
- Pinch of ground nutmeg
- 2tsp cocoa powder
- 1tsp baking powder
- ½tsp bicarbonate of soda
- 200g honey
- 75g butter

TO DECORATE
- 200g plain chocolate
- Edible gold lustre and stars

YOU WILL NEED
- A 6-7cm round biscuit cutter
- 2 baking trays, lined with baking parchment
- A plastic piping bag

★ Preheat oven to gas mark 4/180°C (160°C in a fan oven).

★ Place flour, ground almonds, spices, cocoa powder, baking powder and bicarbonate of soda in a medium bowl.

★ Heat honey and butter together in a pan over a low heat, stirring until the butter melts. Stir into flour and spice mixture until it comes together in a stiff dough. Chill for about 30 mins.

★ Roll out dough on a lightly floured work surface until about 1cm thick, then cut out biscuits with the cutter. Place on baking trays, leaving room between them so they can expand a little. Bake for 15 mins until just beginning to brown on the edges, then leave to cool on a wire rack.

★ **TO DECORATE,** melt chocolate in a bowl over gently simmering water and pour a little over each biscuit until coated. Place remaining chocolate in a piping bag and allow to cool a little until thick enough to pipe. Snip off the end and pipe Christmas designs on to the biscuits, then decorate with gold lustre and stars.

Lemon + coconut SNOWBALLS

These cakes are coated in lemon icing and rolled in coconut. Delicious!

MAKES 12 LARGE OR 24 MINI **PREP** 35 MINS **BAKE** 25 MINS

FOR THE CUPCAKES

- 150g butter
- 150g caster sugar
- 3 eggs, beaten
- 150g self-raising flour
- Zest of 1 lemon

TO DECORATE

- 400g icing sugar
- Juice of ½ lemon
- 200g desiccated coconut

YOU WILL NEED

- A 12-hole cupcake tin or 24-hole mini cupcake tins, lined with paper cases

★ Preheat oven to gas mark 4/180°C (160°C in a fan oven).

★ **TO MAKE CUPCAKES,** place butter and caster sugar in a mixing bowl and beat with a wooden spoon or electric mixer until light and fluffy. Gradually beat in eggs, a little at a time, until smooth, adding a little flour if mixture curdles. Stir in the rest of the flour, as well as the lemon zest, and mix until smooth.

★ Divide mixture between paper cases and bake for 20-25 mins for larger cakes, 12-15 mins for mini ones, or until golden brown and just firm to the touch. Allow to cool on a wire rack.

★ **TO DECORATE,** mix icing sugar with enough lemon juice to make a thick pouring consistency. Remove cupcakes from paper cases and squeeze each cake into a ball shape. Dip into icing, then roll in desiccated coconut. Leave to set.

★ These will keep for 3-4 days in a cake tin.

RECIPE AND FOOD STYLING: MITZIE WILSON PROP STYLING: SUE ROWLANDS PHOTO: TOBY SCOTT

Try this

Make the cakes a day before icing them, or they will be too crumbly to shape and decorate.

Try this
You could also use a chocolate cake or a plain Madeira one, if you prefer.

Let it snow CAKE

This mincemeat loaf is a lovely alternative to Christmas cake.
Decorate it with a snowy icing design

SERVES 8-10 **PREP** 1 HR 30 MINS **BAKE** 1 HR

RECIPE, FOOD AND PROP STYLING: MITZIE WILSON PHOTO: HEARST STUDIOS

TO MAKE THE CAKE

- 200g self-raising flour
- 100g butter
- 75g light muscovado sugar
- 2 eggs
- 300g mincemeat

TO DECORATE

- 2tbsp apricot jam
- 1kg pack ready-to-roll sugar paste
- Pale blue paste food colouring
- Icing sugar, for dusting
- 150g royal icing sugar
- Granulated sugar (optional)

YOU WILL NEED

- A 1kg loaf tin, greased and lined with baking parchment
- A 23cm square cake board
- Alphabet cutters
- Snowflake cutters
- A plastic piping bag

★ Preheat oven to gas mark 4/180°C (160°C in a fan oven).

★ Put flour in a large mixing bowl, add butter and rub in until it forms crumbs. Stir in sugar. Add eggs and mincemeat and beat together until it forms a soft dropping consistency. Spoon into tin.

★ Bake for 1 hr, or until a skewer comes out clean. Leave to cool for 10 mins, then turn out and allow to cool completely.

★ Brush jam all over cake and place on a cake board. Cut off one quarter of the sugar paste and wrap in cling film.

★ Add a little blue food colouring to the rest of the sugar paste and knead until the desired colour. Roll out — on a worktop dusted with icing sugar — into a rectangle large enough to drape over the whole cake. Use to cover cake, letting it fall in soft drapes, and trim away any excess.

★ Roll out remaining sugar paste, then cut out letters with the cutters to form the word 'snow'. Brush the backs of the letters very lightly with boiled water and place on top of cake. Cut out snowflakes with the cutters and attach to the cake, then roll the trimmings into snow balls and arrange around cake.

★ Mix royal icing sugar with just enough water to make a stiff icing. Place in a piping bag, snip off the end and pipe the words 'Let it' above sugar paste letters. Sprinkle granulated sugar over the board, if you like.

★ The cake will keep for 3-4 days in a cake tin.

Meringue TREES

You can store these in a cake tin, ready for a festive party, or serve them as dessert with fresh fruit and cream

MAKES 12   PREP 30 MINS   BAKE 1 HR 30 MINS

FOR THE MERINGUES
- 3 egg whites
- 150g caster sugar
- Sugar sprinkles

YOU WILL NEED
- A large piping bag
- A 2cm star nozzle
- 2 baking trays, lined with baking parchment

★ Preheat oven to gas mark ¼/110°C (90°C in a fan oven).

★ **TO MAKE MERINGUES,** place egg whites and caster sugar in a bowl and whisk with an electric mixer for 10 mins until meringue is smooth, glossy and can stand in firm peaks (use a stand mixer for ease – just set the timer and leave it to do its work).

★ Place mixture in a piping bag fitted with a star nozzle and pipe Christmas-tree shapes on to baking trays. Scatter some sugar sprinkles over each one.

★ Bake meringues for 1 hr 30 mins or until they are dry and firm and come off the baking parchment easily. Turn off the oven and leave them inside to dry a little longer, if you like.

★ These will keep for 1 week in a cake tin.

RECIPE AND FOOD STYLING: MITZIE WILSON PROP STYLING: SUE ROWLANDS PHOTO: TOBY SCOTT

Mini gingerbread bird
HOUSES

Make these sweet little houses to use as edible place settings on the festive table

MAKES 4 **PREP** 2 HRS, PLUS SETTING **BAKE** 15 MINS

RECIPE AND FOOD STYLING: MITZIE WILSON PROP STYLING: SUE ROWLANDS PHOTOS: CLARE WINFIELD

FOR THE GINGERBREAD
- 350g plain flour
- 1tsp bicarbonate of soda
- 2tbsp ground ginger
- 1tbsp ground cinnamon
- 150g butter, chilled and cubed
- 175g light muscovado sugar
- 2tbsp golden syrup
- 1 egg

TO DECORATE
- 250g royal icing sugar
- Blue sugar crystals
- Red edible glitter

YOU WILL NEED
- Card for the template
- A 10cm round cutter
- 2 or 3 baking trays, lined with baking parchment
- Piping bags and nozzles
- A small white cardboard lollipop stick, cut to fit (as a perch)
- Red food colouring

★ Preheat oven to gas mark 4/180°C (160°C in a fan oven).

★ **TO MAKE GINGERBREAD,** mix flour, bicarbonate of soda, ginger and cinnamon together. Rub in butter with your fingertips.

★ Stir in sugar, syrup and egg. Using your hands, knead mixture together in a bowl until smooth, then refrigerate to firm up.

★ Meanwhile, make the template. Cut a rectangle of card 6cm x 5cm for the sides of the house, a rectangle 8cm x 4cm for the roof, and a rectangle, 6cm x 7.5cm for the gable ends. To make a gable shape, fold the card in half along 6cm edge, measure 5.5cm up the long edge, then cut diagonally from this mark to the gable's centre point, and open out the card.

★ Roll out gingerbread and use templates to cut out 8 sides, 8 roof pieces and 8 gable ends. Make a hole in 4 gable ends using a small piping nozzle and make a small hole for the perch using the point of an icing tube. Re-roll trimmings and cut out 4 x 10cm circles of dough (for the bases) and 4 small bird shapes. Place all gingerbread on baking trays and bake for 10-12 mins or until they are tinged brown at the edge. Leave to cool for 10 mins, then place on a wire rack to cool completely. The pieces can be stored in a cake tin for up to 1 week before assembly.

★ **TO DECORATE,** make up the royal icing as directed on pack. Spread roof pieces with royal icing and dip into blue sugar crystals.

★ Place some icing in a piping bag. Colour a small amount of icing red and put in another piping bag. Snip off the ends. Pipe a pattern around the hole in the gable and add the lollipop stick as a perch, securing with icing. Pipe a line along the base of 1 side piece, press on to a base and prop up to make a side. Use icing to glue the remaining pieces in place, propping them up if necessary. Allow sides to set for a few minutes before adding the roof. Pipe on decorations.

★ Place icing on the breast of the bird, dip in red glitter and pipe on a small eye. Glue on a piece of orange peel with icing for a beak, if you like. Leave to set overnight.

Mini PANETTONES

*A little effort is well worth it in the end
for these rich Italian-style cakes*

MAKES 12 **PREP** 30 MINS, PLUS PROVING **BAKE** 25 MINS

FIRST DOUGH
- 150g strong white bread flour
- ½tsp salt
- 2tsp easy bake yeast
- 2tbsp caster sugar
- 25g butter
- 1 egg

SECOND DOUGH
- 125g strong white bread flour
- 50g butter, at room temperature, diced
- 50g caster sugar
- 1 egg and 2 egg yolks
- Zest of 1 orange
- 100g plain chocolate, chopped
- 75g candied orange peel, chopped

YOU WILL NEED
- 12 tulip muffin cases (from Lakeland)

★ Preheat oven to gas mark 5/190°C (170°C in a fan oven).

★ **TO MAKE FIRST DOUGH,** add flour, salt, yeast and sugar to a bowl and rub in butter, then stir in egg. Warm 100ml water until hand-hot, then stir into the mixture, beating to a smooth, thick dough. Cover with cling film and leave in a warm place until doubled in size – this can take up to 45 minutes.

★ **TO MAKE SECOND DOUGH,** mix all the ingredients together and leave to one side. When the first dough has risen and is full of bubbles, add second dough to it and mix well.

★ Divide mixture between muffin cases, cover with oiled cling film and leave until doubled in size again.

★ Bake for 20-25 mins until they have risen and are golden brown.

★ These are best eaten on the day they are made.

RECIPE AND FOOD STYLING: MITZIE WILSON PROP STYLING: SUE ROWLANDS PHOTO: TOBY SCOTT

Try this

Make dough in 2 batches so the yeast can ferment quickly, without being inhibited by the richness of the eggs and butter.

Orange + cranberry
HEART

This orange-flavoured cake is topped with chocolate twigs and wafers for an outdoors feel

SERVES 8 **PREP** 1 HR **BAKE** 30 MINS

RECIPE AND FOOD STYLING: MITZIE WILSON **PROP STYLING:** SUE ROWLANDS **PHOTO:** TOBY SCOTT

FOR THE CAKE
- 150g caster sugar
- 150g butter, softened
- 3 eggs, beaten
- 150g self-raising flour
- Zest of 1 orange
- Few drops of orange extract (optional)
- 100g dried cranberries

FOR THE ICING
- 100g butter, softened
- 250g icing sugar, plus extra for dusting
- Pinch of ground cinnamon

FOR THE DECORATION
- A mixture of chocolate twigs, chocolate pretzels and wafer curls
- 50g each green and red sugar paste
- Cocoa powder, to dust

YOU WILL NEED
- A 750ml heart-shaped cake tin, greased and lined with baking parchment
- A small ivy cutter

★ Preheat oven to gas mark 4/180°C (160°C in a fan oven).

★ **FOR THE CAKE,** place sugar and butter in a mixing bowl and beat with a wooden spoon or electric mixer until light and fluffy. Gradually beat in eggs, a little at a time, until smooth – adding a little flour if the mixture starts to curdle.

★ Stir in the remaining flour, as well as the orange zest and extract, if using, and dried cranberries.

★ Add cake mixture to the tin and bake for 25-30 mins until golden brown and just firm to the touch. Allow to cool on a wire rack, then remove the parchment.

★ **TO MAKE THE ICING,** beat together butter, icing sugar and cinnamon until smooth, adding a drop of boiling water, if necessary. Spread over cake, then arrange twigs, pretzels and wafer curls on top.

★ Roll out green sugar paste on a work surface dusted with icing sugar. Cut out ivy leaves and roll thin sausages of icing for the stems. Dust cocoa over the cake and arrange the stems, ivy leaves and little balls of red sugar paste on top.

RECIPE AND FOOD STYLING: MITZIE WILSON PROP STYLING: SUE ROWLANDS PHOTO: TOBY SCOTT

Try this
You can use a mixture of any dried fruit, or instead of marshmallows, try chopped honeycomb.

Rocky road
CHUNKS

These are sure to be a hit – so make plenty for everyone to tuck in, or package them up to take to a friend

MAKES 16 CHUNKS **PREP** 15 MINS, PLUS SETTING **BAKE** NONE

TO MAKE THE CHUNKS

- 100g butter
- 200g plain chocolate
- 2tbsp golden syrup
- 75g dried cranberries
- 100g white chocolate chips
- 100g mini marshmallows
- 200g chopped biscuits
(eg wafers, amaretti, shortbread or digestives)

YOU WILL NEED

- A 20cm square cake tin, lined with baking parchment

★ Place butter, chocolate and syrup in a pan over a gentle heat and melt gently. Stir until smooth, then allow to cool until it is no longer hot when you dip your finger in it.

★ Stir in the remaining ingredients, then tip it all into the cake tin. Chill in the fridge for a couple of hours to allow it to set, then turn out and cut into chunks.

★ This will keep for up to 2 weeks in the fridge.

JUST £3
FOR 3 ISSUES*

Prima provides real-life guidance, inspiration and ideas to simplify the lives of modern women today. It's packed with tips, tricks and clever ideas on the key elements in your life and brings you time- and money-saving solutions to make your month run smoothly.

Great reasons to subscribe

- **ONLY £1** a copy for your first 3 issues* (normal price £3.10)
- **SAVE 35%** on every issue thereafter**
- **FREE** Prima pattern with every issue††
- **EXCLUSIVE** subscriber-only offers and competitions

FREE PRIMA PATTERN WITH EVERY ISSUE††

HOW TO SUBSCRIBE
Order online – it's fast and simple
hearstmagazines.co.uk/pr/KPRBAKE
Call **0844 848 1601**† TODAY and quote offer code KPR10375

†BT landline calls to 0844 numbers will cost no more than 5p per minute; calls from mobiles and other networks usually cost more.

CONVERSION TABLES

WEIGHT

grams/KG	oz/lbs
25g	1oz
50g	2oz
75g	3oz
125g	4oz
150g	5oz
175g	6oz
200g	7oz
225g	8oz
250g	9oz
275g	10oz
300g	11oz
350g	12oz
375g	13oz
400g	14oz
425g	15oz
450g	1lb
550g	1¼lb
700g	1½lb
900g	2lb
1.1kg	2½lb
1.4kg	3lb
1.6kg	3½lb
1.8kg	4lb
2kg	4½lb
2.3kg	5lb

VOLUME

ml/litres	fl oz/pints
25ml	1fl oz
50ml	2fl oz
150ml	5fl oz (¼pt)
200ml	7fl oz (⅓pt)
300ml	10fl oz (½pt)
450ml	15fl oz (¾pt)
500-600ml	20fl oz (1pt)
750ml	1¼pt
900ml	1½pt
1l	1¾pt
1.1l	2pt
1.3l	2¼pt
1.4l	2½pt
1.6l	2¾pt
1.7l	3pt

SPOONS

ml	tsp/tbsp
1.25ml	¼tsp
2.5ml	½tsp
3.75ml	¾tsp
5ml	1tsp
15ml	1tbsp

Try this

Always use the same measurements for an entire recipe – don't mix metric and imperial.

OVEN TEMPERATURES

Gas mark	°C	°C in a fan oven
¼	110	90
½	130	110
1	140	120
2	150	130
3	170	150
4	180	160
5	190	170
6	200	180
7	220	200
8	230	210
9	240	220

Cook's notes